CHER HAMPTON

Overcoming Anxious Attachment

*A 3-step Healing Journey to Emotional Freedom,
Finding Love and Security, and Building Healthy
Relationships*

Contents

BONUS: Your Free Gift

I'm only offering these bonuses for FREE to my readers. This is a way of saying thanks for your purchase. In this gift, you will find a guide with extra tools to start your inner journey and a self-development course.

Healing your Inner Child First Guide

Inside this book, you'll discover:

1. How to use Journaling in the Healing Process.
2. Questions to Remember Your Inner Child.
3. Space to Write Your Thoughts Down.
4. Questions to Better Understand Your Inner Child's Pain.
5. Motivational Things to Say to Your Inner Child.
6. Positive Affirmations + a 5-Step Method to Make Your Own.
7. An Extra Inner Child Meditation.
8. A Checklist.
9. And More…

The Personality Development Wisdom Mini Course

Inside this theoretical and video course, you will find:

1. Personality Development - An Overview
2. How to Transform Yourself into a Better Version
3. How To Improve Your Body Language
4. How to Boost Up Your Self-Confidence, Self-Esteem, and Motivation
5. Best Tips to Overcome Procrastination
6. The Power of Positive Thinking
7. How to Improve Your Workplace Wellness
8. How to Enhance Your Softskill
9. Learn and Practice the Art of Work-Life Balance
10. How to Deal With Failures
11. How to Manage and Overcome Your Fears
12. Best Ways to Deal With Difficult People
13. Stress and Energy Management
14. How to Have a Productive Day
15. Bonus 1 - Cheat Sheet
16. Bonus 2 - Mind Map
17. Bonus 3 - Top Resource Report
18. Bonus 4 - 10 Extra Articles

To receive these extra **bonuses,** go to: https://booksforbetterlife.com/innerchild

Or scan the QR code:

About The Author

Cher Hampton is an author and developmental psychologist, born and raised in the United States. She grew up with her mother and stepfather, as her parents divorced when she was one year old. She is also the older sibling to one younger sister from her father and one younger brother from her mother.

Cher grew up with a mother that suffered from bipolar disorder. On top of that, when she was seven years old, her stepfather committed suicide. The combination of these circumstances made her develop and mature very early in life and did not give her the opportunity to be a child as she was supposed to be.

Following this, she suffered from depression and burnout during her teen years. During these years, signs of her anxious attachment started to become visible. She lacked trust in herself, had poor self-esteem, feared being abandoned, and had an obsessive need for approval.

Unbeknownst to her, she was also forming unhealthy relationships, even at her own cost, by having an exaggerated sense of responsibility for the actions of others. But this didn't make her feel any safer in these relationships because instead of wanting to be emotionally close, she avoided connecting with others. Constant thoughts of not being good enough and trouble expressing her feelings led to shallow, short-lived, and unfulfilling relationships.

As a young adult, after going through many years of psychotherapy, she was committed to healing herself. She decided to study for a degree in psychology to learn more about her psyche and help others to do the same. Today, Cher is a trained psychologist and is determined to reach as many people as possible with her collection of books and knowledge.

Introduction

"A securely attached child will store an internal working model of a responsive, loving, reliable care-giver, and of a self that is worthy of love and attention and will bring these assumptions to bear on all other relationships."

— JEREMY HOLMES

We all desire to feel loved and appreciated by others. This is because when we are in the company of those who love us, our basic human need for safety is fulfilled. However, as comforting as feeling loved can be, it is also a terrifying experience for those who have developed anxious attachment.

Nobody chooses to be anxiously attached to people. If it were a choice, perhaps everybody would have gone with secure attachment. However, our attachment styles are created from the early relationships we formed in life, particularly the mother-child relationship.

An adult who both desires and fears love was once a child who received hot and cold parenting. One minute their parent was emotionally present and affectionate, then the next minute they were dismissive and withdrawn. Since survival was on the line, the child had to learn how to cope with these inconsistencies, and that is how they developed anxious attachment.

You have picked up this book because to some degree, you have been exposed to someone or perhaps have lived with anxious attachment for all of your life. You may be able to relate to the experience of receiving hot and cold treatment from your parent and growing up feeling insecure about who you are and where your place is in the world.

During moments in your childhood when you needed love the most, you could not find it. The unspoken message that you internalized was *Love is complicated*. Little did you know how much the attachment formed with your parent, and all of the harmful beliefs and coping mechanisms you adopted back then, would reinforce the same relational patterns in future relationships.

The purpose of this book is to take a deep dive into the anxious attachment style, which is explained in the attachment theory discovered by psychologists John Bowlby and Mary Ainsworth (Bretherton, 1992). This type of attachment is a result of inconsistent parenting patterns that cause a child to develop a deep sense of rejection and suffer with a low self-esteem.

Not only will we explore the origins and causes of anxious attachment, but we will also look at how it can affect relationship building and cultivating a strong sense of self as an adult. The takeaway message from this book should be that anxious attachment can be healed through introspection, reparenting, and discovering your sense of self-worth.

How to Use This Book

This book is your guide to healing anxious attachment and developing a deeper appreciation for yourself. The book is divided into three parts, namely:

Part 1: Recognizing Anxious Attachment
Part 2: Confronting Anxious Attachment
Part 3: Reconnecting With Yourself

The final chapter will include exercises, meditations, and journal prompts to help you practice the various strategies discussed throughout the book.

Please note that due to the nature of the subject, some examples included in the book may be triggering for sensitive readers.

I

Recognizing Anxious Attachment

1

The Four Attachment Styles

"Some of us wonder if we can feel secure without being abandoned and some of us wonder if we can feel secure without being overwhelmed. Some of us a little of both."

— ALLYSON DINNEEN

In this chapter you will learn:

- How the parent-child bond is formed
- The origins of attachment theory and how attachment styles develop
- How to identify your attachment style

The Bond That Begins in the Womb

The unspoken bond between a mother and her child begins in the womb. Even though the fetus cannot see its mother, it can respond to touch and emotions. If you read birth stories, you will hear of mothers who bond with their unborn children by massaging their bellies, singing, or reading children's books. To show that they are paying attention, the children might respond by kicking back or changing positions.

Research has also shown that children begin to intuitively pick up on their parents' emotions while inside the womb. When a mother is upset, for example, the child's heart rate can double.

This doesn't usually have a negative effect on the child when the negative emotions felt by the mother happen once in a while. However, if the mother is in severe distress for a good portion of her pregnancy, the constant stress felt by the child can impact their personality and continued development outside the womb (Sorgen, n.d.).

The reason why it is important to speak about life inside the womb is because that is where the mother-child bond begins. Being able to lovingly respond to the nudges of the unborn child and create a safe environment for them to grow is the first sign or evidence of love and what the child can look forward to outside the womb.

Babies can see, feel, taste, hear, and think before birth. The question for mothers is: *What thoughts, emotions, or memories about your connection will the newborn come into the world with?*

Attachment Outside the Womb

An attachment is an emotional connection between two people that is seen by the way they interact with each other. Newborns form attachments with their birth parents or caregivers who provide for their needs.

It is important to make a distinction between attachment and genuine love since these terms tend to be used interchangeably. The main point to emphasize is that children form attachments with their caregivers out of necessity. Since they cannot survive in the world without being fed, burped, changed, or put to sleep, the care they receive from their primary caregivers creates a strong connection—regardless of the presence of affection and nurturing.

Love is a feeling that is formed separately.

There are some parents who develop love for their newborns and others who don't. When an attachment is formed without love, taking care of the child becomes no more than a duty. The parent knows they are responsible for raising their child, but they don't have any genuine feelings of love that inspire them to be selflessly devoted to parenting.

A sign of a healthy attachment is the presence of love, and an unhealthy attachment the absence of it. One way that we can identify the presence of love between parents and children is to see if the parents are "moved" by their children. In other words, do they respond timeously and appropriately to the children's needs?

Relationship researcher Dr. John Gottman believes that in healthy and loving relationships, both parties will respond favorably to each other's bids for connection. He goes on to describe a bid as "an attempt to get attention, affection, or acceptance" (Eanes, 2016).

For older children, the question "Will you play with me?" is a direct bid to connect, which can be answered with a yes or no (i.e. accepting or declining the bid). But for newborns and toddlers who are not able to verbalize their bids, crying, smiling, or making eye contact are ways in which they attempt to connect with their parents. There are three ways parents can respond to these bids:

- turning toward the child and responding to the bid
- turning away from the child and dismissing the bid
- turning against the child and showing no response or action at all

For example, a toddler who is visibly upset might crawl up to their mother and signal to be picked up. This signal is a bid to connect and receive their mother's affection and reassurance. In response, the mother can respond in three ways:

1. **Turning toward:** Mirror the child's facial expressions, pick them up, and offer a warm hug.
2. **Turning away:** Give the child a puzzled look and tell them to stop crying.
3. **Turning against:** Avoid eye contact with the child and continue to work on the task they were busy with.

Circling back to the connection between love and attachment, parents who turn toward their children and respond to their bids make them feel loved and nurtured. However, those who turn away from or against their children can make them feel unloved and insecure. Note that it takes numerous missed opportunities to connect to make children feel unloved. In other words, there must be a pattern or habit of ignoring children's bids to create an unhealthy attachment.

Attachment Theory

Whenever the topic of attachment is brought up, you will hear the mention of attachment theory. In the field of psychology, attachment theory is often used to explain the emotional bonds between people, particularly the bond between a mother and child.

John Bowlby was the first psychologist to write on attachments. In his work, he described them as psychological connectedness between human beings (Bowlby, 1969). Bowlby wanted to understand why children would become anxious or distressed when separated from their parents. He learned that separation anxiety was caused by distinct behavioral patterns.

A year later, a second psychologist, Mary Ainsworth, expanded on Bowlby's work in a famous study that explored the effects of early attachment on children's behaviors. The participants were mothers with children between 12 to 18 months old. They were given the instruction to leave their babies in a room for a brief moment, before reuniting. Based on the results of the study, Ainsworth identified three attachment styles: secure, ambivalent-insecure, and avoidant-insecure (Ainsworth & Bell, 1970). A few years later, two researchers, Main and Solomon, wrote a chapter about a fourth attachment style they called disorganized-insecure, in a book titled *Affective Development in Infancy* (Brazelton & Yogman, 1986).

There have been countless studies undertaken to support and explain how these four attachment styles impact relationship building later in life. Below is a brief introduction to each attachment style and some of their characteristics.

Secure Attachment

Secure attachment occurs when caregivers are able to respond and validate their children's needs. This enables children to confidently express their thoughts and feelings and develop a stable identity. The hallmark of secure attachment is emotional availability and providing children with positive reinforcement. Other signs of secure attachment include:

- good emotional regulation
- high self-esteem
- easily trusting others
- effective communication skills
- the ability to set healthy boundaries
- the ability to self-reflect in relationships

In adulthood: While secure attachment is the ideal style of attachment in any relationship, it isn't perfect. For instance, those who have secure attachments can experience relationship struggles like anybody else. However, the difference is that they are more psychologically equipped to handle the highs and lows of relationships.

Ambivalent-Insecure Attachment

Ambivalence-insecure attachment, also known as anxious attachment, occurs when children receive inconsistent parenting. This creates a push and pull dynamic between caregivers and their children, which causes children to feel insecure. Some of the consequences of developing this type of attachment are forming an unstable identity, developing a fear of rejection or abandonment, or seeking constant reassurance from others. Other signs of ambivalent-insecure attachment that can manifest include:

- sensitive to real or perceived rejection/criticism
- developing clingy or needy tendencies
- low self-esteem
- difficulty trusting others
- feeling unworthy of love

In adulthood: What makes this style of attachment interesting is how it creates an intense desire and fear of affection and intimacy. On the one hand, someone might yearn for their romantic partner's embrace, but once they have it, they might feel smothered or deeply unsettled. The familiar push and pull dynamic learned from the earlier relationship with their parents informs their ability to give and receive love later on.

Avoidant-Insecure Attachment

Avoidant-insecure attachment, also known as avoidant-dismissive attachment, occurs when caregivers have been absent or neglectful during their children's upbringing. Instead of feeling insecure about affection or intimacy (as with the ambivalent-insecure attachment), children grow up being fearful or dismissive of them. The pain of emotionally unavailable parents can be harbored by children until adulthood. Some of the signs of this style of attachment include:

- pattern of avoiding physical or emotional intimacy
- unconsciously sabotaging romantic or platonic relationships
- fear of expressing strong emotions
- feeling threatened by people who want to connect
- developing a fear of commitment

In adulthood: Some mistakenly believe that people with this style of attachment are incapable of giving or receiving love. The truth is that they don't have "love issues" but rather trust issues. It is their chronic mistrust of others that makes them reject any signs of intimacy or connection. Working through these trust issues can significantly improve their relationships.

Disorganized-Insecure Attachment

Disorganized-insecure attachment occurs when children develop an unstable relationship with their caregivers due to being exposed to abuse, trauma, alcoholism, or mental illness. For instance, a child raised by an alcoholic parent may have had to assume the parental role and mature ahead of time, in order to take care of their younger siblings or the household. Having this type of parent-child relationship confuses the child and causes both symptoms of anxious and avoidant attachment. The child may also experience:

- fear of rejection
- high levels of anxiety
- unstable sense of self
- poor emotional regulation

In adulthood: In most cases, people who develop this style of attachment were exposed to early childhood trauma, either at the hands of their parents or with their parents' knowledge. They may experience similar outcomes as those with anxious or avoidant attachment styles and may also be vulnerable to mental illness like substance abuse disorder, mood disorders, or eating disorders.

Can You Heal From Your Attachment Style?

Children who aren't able to form secure attachments with their caregivers develop psychological wounds. They may be able to forget the memories of being neglected by their parents, but the pain of that emotional disconnect is very much alive in their subconscious minds.

The big question is: Can adults heal from the early attachments formed with their parents? The answer is yes; however, there is a lot of inner work required to recognize and process childhood psychological wounds. The purpose of this book is to focus on identifying and healing anxious attachment, which is possible through applying a variety of interventions, including psychotherapy, making healthy lifestyle choices, and embracing spirituality.

Quiz: Discover Your Attachment Style

You may or may not have an idea about which attachment style you fall under. This quiz is a fun activity to familiarize you with each style of attachment.

The tables present four styles of attachment. Go through each table and consider how much you agree with the statements. Place a tick inside the appropriate column, then tally your score after completing the table. The table with the highest score will likely represent the style of attachment you resonate with most.

Table 1: Secure Attachment

Statement	Disagree	Sometimes Agree	Mostly Agree	Strongly Agree
I feel at ease in my relationships most of the time.	0	1	2	3
I am comfortable being alone just as much as I enjoy being with others.	0	1	2	3
When I get into conflict with others, I am able to self-reflect and apologize if I was in the wrong.	0	1	2	3
I believe that, in general, human beings are naturally good hearted.	0	1	2	3
I honor commitments made with other people most of the time.	0	1	2	3
I seek to fulfill the needs of my loved ones, and I am confident expressing my own needs.	0	1	2	3
I am protective over my loved ones and seek to maintain physical and emotional safety in our relationships.	0	1	2	3
I have a positive perception of the people that matter most to me.	0	1	2	3
I enjoy physical touch and intimacy with my partner.	0	1	2	3
I take my partner's boundaries seriously.	0	1	2	3
Section Total:				

Table 2: Ambivalent-Insecure Attachment				
Statement	Disagree	Sometimes Agree	Mostly Agree	Strongly Agree
I am constantly longing for someone or something that I cannot have.	0	1	2	3
I tend to be over-accommodating or over-apologize in relationships to keep the connection stable.	0	1	2	3
I tend to lose myself in relationships because of being overly focused on others.	0	1	2	3
I struggle to say "no" to others or set healthy boundaries.	0	1	2	3
I tend to second-guess myself and wish I had done or said things differently.	0	1	2	3
I secretly harbor resentment when I give more than I receive.	0	1	2	3
I try to avoid being alone because it makes me feel hurt, stressed, or abandoned.	0	1	2	3
I have a chronic fear of being abandoned by my romantic partner.	0	1	2	3
As much as I love to be around my romantic partner, I sometimes pick fights to test the strength of the relationship.	0	1	2	3
I unconsciously take on the mannerisms and personality traits of my romantic partner.	0	1	2	3
Section Total:				

Table 3: Avoidant-Insecure Attachment

Statement	Disagree	Sometimes Agree	Mostly Agree	Strongly Agree
When others request to spend time with me, I feel inexplicably stressed.	0	1	2	3
I tend to downplay the importance of close relationships in my life.	0	1	2	3
I struggle to ask for help from others. I believe in being self-reliant.	0	1	2	3
I feel a sense of relief in not needing other people.	0	1	2	3
I need to have plenty of time and space to myself in relationships.	0	1	2	3
Sometimes I prefer to have casual sex than a fully committed relationship.	0	1	2	3
I feel less anxious in relationships with animals or things like work or hobbies.	0	1	2	3
I dislike many forms of intimacy like holding hands or making eye contact.	0	1	2	3
I tend to rationalize my emotions instead of feeling them.	0	1	2	3
I feel a sense of freedom when I break up with a romantic partner, which is followed by depressive emotions.	0	1	2	3
Section Total:				

Table 4: Disorganized-Insecure Attachment

Statement	Disagree	Sometimes Agree	Mostly Agree	Strongly Agree
When I develop a strong emotional connection with others, I feel a sense of fear.	0	1	2	3
When I am faced with problems, I tend to freeze and feel hopeless.	0	1	2	3
I get startled easily, especially when others approach me unexpectedly.	0	1	2	3
Friends and family often express that I am controlling.	0	1	2	3
I tend to expect the worst to happen in my relationships.	0	1	2	3
I struggle to feel safe and relaxed in romantic relationships.	0	1	2	3
I have difficulty remembering past memories related to my attachment issues.	0	1	2	3
Even though I desire closeness, I struggle to make the effort to get to know people.	0	1	2	3
I fail to protect myself when faced with threatening situations.	0	1	2	3
Since I tend to freeze or disconnect when feeling stressed, I prefer simple and clear communication.	0	1	2	3
Section Total:				

Key Takeaways

- The parent-child bond begins in the womb through the mother's responsiveness to her unborn child.
- Psychologists John Bowlby and Mary Ainsworth are attributed for creating what we know today as the attachment theory. The theory seeks to explain the various emotional bonds children can form with their caregivers.
- Every child develops an attachment to their parents out of the need to survive, but this doesn't always mean that the attachment is healthy.
- From an early age, children make bids for affection by seeking their mother's attention. Genuine love between a parent and child is formed when the mother is willing and enthusiastic about responding to bids.

2

How Attachment Styles Affect Relationships

"The key to finding a mate who can fulfill those needs is to first fully acknowledge your need for intimacy, availability, and security in a relationship—and to believe that they are legitimate."

— AMIR LEVINE & RACHEL S.F. HELLER

In this chapter you will learn:

- How attachment styles affect different areas of your life
- The barriers that anxious, avoidant, and disorganized attachment create with communication, empathy, intimacy, and stress management

Everyday Interactions With Different Attachment Styles

Jane has a secure attachment style. She was raised by emotionally available parents, who offered a predictable and structured environment with regular positive reinforcement. Growing up, Jane didn't have difficulty building and maintaining friendships. However, she also didn't feel obliged to keep friendships that were no longer mutually beneficial. Her openness to express needs and wants allowed her to communicate healthy boundaries and hold others accountable to them. In the face of rejection or invalidation, she was able to set limits, issue consequences, and quickly restabilize herself.

Timothy has an ambivalent-insecure attachment style. He was raised by a single mother who worked two jobs and often left the role of parenting to different babysitters. There is no doubt that Timothy was dearly loved by his mother, but he often yearned for her attention and affection.

Since his emotional needs were neglected as a child, he grew up seeking relationships that will fill that inner void. Once attached to an individual, he would become clingy and codependent. At the back of his mind, he feared losing close relationships because his identity was wrapped up in them. He often wondered how he would survive without the people he cared about most.

Mariah has an avoidant-insecure attachment style. She was raised in a traditional and strict household by parents who were ex-military officers. Her parents were not affectionate or emotionally expressive; they showed love by providing a safe and predictable lifestyle, as well as rewarding good behaviors.

Growing up, Mariah struggled to share her thoughts and feelings openly with her parents, out of fear of being judged or misunderstood. This pattern continued into adulthood and caused communication and intimacy problems in her relationships. While she desired love and closeness, she was very uncomfortable with it, and often preferred shallow and less intense connections.

Sonia has a disorganized-insecure attachment style. She was raised in a dysfunctional home environment where substance abuse was rampant with both parents. Growing up, Sonia never developed a healthy bond with her parents. She learned to protect herself by creating two different personas; one that was hard and emotionless and another that was authentic and trusting.

In adult relationships, these two personas often appeared together and created confusion and drama. People often didn't know "which Sonia" they were going to get whenever they interacted with her. Sonia felt the same frustration not being able to let go of her defensiveness and seek closeness. She believed that perhaps there were underlying mental health problems that were also keeping her from establishing a healthy sense of self.

Your attachment style begins with your early caregivers, but ultimately affects platonic, romantic, and professional relationships you will form later in life. Before starting the process of healing your attachment style, it is important to consider the various ways it can impact the quality of your relationships. What follows are five aspects of relationships that are influenced by attachment styles.

Communication

Communication skills are an essential part of human development. Without being able to clearly communicate what you are thinking and feeling to others, you won't be able to meet your needs.

Being a good communicator isn't based on simply talking. If that was the case, then there wouldn't be such a thing as misunderstandings. In order for talking to be effective, your messages must be expressed with clarity and honesty. Unfortunately, your attachment style can get in the way of how you talk and get your messages across to others.

For instance, secure types are known to be straightforward communicators. They may not always express themselves appropriately, but they are able to reflect on their thoughts and emotions and share them with others. This ability enables them to set boundaries, notify others when boundaries have been broken, and negotiate a positive way forward.

Anxious types spend more time attempting to figure out what others are thinking and feeling, which makes them detached from their own thoughts and feelings. It is common for them to be confused about what they want, and this delays their needs being met. Since anxious types are also prone to be people-pleasers, they are likely to say whatever they believe others want to hear, rather than openly stating their opinions—especially when they believe stating their opinions can lead to conflict or judgment.

Avoidant-insecure types can easily be triggered by what others think and feel. They will typically be dismissive of others when they are told something that they don't approve of. Dismissive behavior may include yelling, using threatening language, or giving the silent treatment. Since avoidant-insecure types are sensitive to negative emotions, they may also find it difficult to accept when they have been hurt by others. It is easier for them to suppress their emotions and simply ignore or move away from the wrongdoer.

Disorganized types tend to adopt the same communication behaviors as anxious and avoidant-insecure people. However, what is particularly unique about this type is that they tend to crave connection but become equally stressed in close relationships. They may find it difficult to express their needs, even when it is in their best interest to (e.g. when their basic human needs are in jeopardy).

Empathy

Empathy is a personality trait that describes the ability to show compassion for other people's experiences. It seeks to help you understand what others may be thinking or feeling and the emotional impact of their circumstances.

Generally speaking, human beings are not born empathetic. This trait is usually taught through interactions with caregivers. For example, from a young age, parents can teach empathy by creating an emotionally safe space for their children to express their thoughts and feelings at home and using validating language as part of everyday communication.

A 2012 study found that attachment styles could predict whether or not people were inclined to be empathetic. The study invited 260 nursing students, both male and female, and they were asked to fill out the Interpersonal Reactivity Index (IRI) and the Attachment Style Questionnaire (ASQ). The results from the study showed that students with secure attachment had a positive correlation with empathy, while students with insecure attachment styles (including both ambivalent-insecure and avoidant-insecure attachment) had a negative correlation with empathy (Khodabakhsh, 2012).

Note that findings like these don't suggest that those with insecure attachment styles cannot be empathetic; however, they may struggle to display empathy due to being low in openness. Moreover, it is worth considering that since people with insecure attachment styles struggled to form safe and close bonds with caregivers at a young age, they are more likely to shy away from getting too close to others. Seeing other people express negative emotions could also be something that makes them feel uncomfortable.

Another interesting aspect of empathy is compassion, which is the act of being kind and supportive of others. In order to show compassion, one must first be compassionate to themselves, which means being good at responding to one's own needs. Since those with insecure attachment styles tend to develop a pattern of repressing their needs, self-care is an area that is typically lacking in their lives. This makes it harder for them to respond to the needs of others.

While ambivalent-insecure types can pour from an empty cup and overextend themselves to others, this shouldn't be seen as an example of compassion. If we study the intentions of their seemingly selfless giving, we will see that ambivalent-insecure types extend themselves to others from a place of fear, rather than love (e.g. fear of ruining their reputation or losing a loved one). Avoidant-insecure types, on the other hand, won't attempt to win the favor of others. Their feelings of inner emptiness drive their flighty and dismissive behaviors.

Intimacy

Intimacy can be described as a feeling of closeness, sometimes sexual in nature, within interpersonal relationships. Building healthy intimacy takes time and a great deal of trust. However, the reward of this is that you can feel safe and free to express yourself in relationships.

Those with secure attachment are often raised in loving and child-friendly environments that allow them to feel safe expressing their needs and wants and making bids for affection to their caregivers. Knowing that they can trust their caregivers to behave consistently, regardless of how they might feel toward them, creates a powerful bond. It also boosts their self-confidence and cultivates a healthy sense of self-worth. As adults, securely attached people will display low levels of anxiety and avoidance in relationships. They are also less likely to use sex as a way to "buy" affection or boost their self-esteem.

The other attachment styles (i.e. ambivalent-insecure, avoidant-insecure, and disorganized-insecure) are also capable of developing intimacy, but the difference is that it tends to look and feel unhealthy. A pop culture term that describes this type of unhealthy intimacy is "toxic love."

Those with ambivalent-insecure attachment crave healthy intimacy but are also deathly afraid of it. They are the type of people who will fantasize about being in loving and committed romantic relationships, but they will unconsciously sabotage their unions through codependent behaviors or distrusting their partners. What makes them behave in this way?

As children, their experience of love was hot and cold. They could

23

never fully relax in the parent-child relationship because unexpectedly, the bond would be tested. For instance, their parents would pull away, become emotionally abusive, or become preoccupied with something or someone they deemed more important. A parent who was a workaholic could have spent more time at work than home, or one who was in a codependent romantic relationship could have prioritized their partner over their child.

In adult relationships, ambivalent-insecure types tend to obsess about closeness and worry excessively about whether their relationships will last. This can make them self-conscious, jealous, and codependent. Moreover, they often struggle to trust others fully, which affects their ability to form healthy intimacy. What they believe to be "true love" could in some cases be neediness or dependency.

Avoidant-insecure people treat intimacy differently. They do not fantasize about closeness, nor do they desire that kind of bond with others. The idea of being vulnerable and allowing others to know them on a deeper level is off putting. The reason they behave in this way can also be traced back to the parent-child relationship. As children, avoidant types were not shown open displays of affection and nurturing, such as being comforted with hugs, kissed on the cheek, or told "I love you." For this reason, they grew up being weary of relationships that require emotional investment.

In adult relationships, avoidant types prefer casual sexual encounters and easy-going shallow connections over long-term commitment. They tend to view partners who seek intimacy as being overly needy and demanding too much out of them. Additionally, they may fear their sense of independence being threatened when sharing space or being too close to others. Similar to anxious types, they can also sabotage relationships by giving into their fears.

Lastly, people with disorganized-insecure attachment tend to reflect anxious and avoidant tendencies when getting close to others. These behaviors are caused by a low self-esteem and a sense of unworthiness to being loved. Similar to avoidant types, they prefer to have shallow friendships or casual sexual encounters instead of being in deeply committed relationships.

Stress Management

Research has shown how early childhood attachment impacts the body's physiological and psychological response to stress (Munger, n.d.). The stress response, also known as "fight flight freeze mode," is a trigger that is activated whenever the brain perceives threats. There are usually three primal responses or reactions that ensue: attack, run away, or freeze.

However, when we study attachment theory, we can see the various ways that people react in stressful situations, such as:

- how one perceives stress in challenging situations
- how one reacts at the moment, as well as how one recovers from a stressful situation
- the effect that friends and family have on helping one cope with stress
- the various coping strategies that one uses to adapt to ongoing stressful situations

Secure types, for example, cope with stress by proactively looking for solutions, leaning on loved ones, or taking a different perspective.

These coping strategies reduce feelings of fear and panic and encourage logical thinking. Of course, this doesn't mean that people with secure attachment don't overreact. Just like any human being, they can sometimes react negatively to stress or unforeseen events. Nevertheless, their overreaction is short-lived due to their solutions-based approach to stress management. Typical phrases that a secure person might say when feeling stressed are "I'm so disappointed, but I will get through this" or "I am feeling overwhelmed. I need to speak with someone."

Ambivalent-insecure types almost anticipate stressful events, even when there are no signs of threats in their environment. In fact, many anxious people will create worst-case scenarios in their minds to justify their anxious feelings. For example, when they notice that a loved one's cell phone has been off the entire morning, they might assume they are in danger. This scenario can feel so real in their minds that it triggers a panic and interferes with their productivity.

Calm or stable situations often feel "too good to be true" for someone with ambivalent-insecure attachment. In relationships, this can sometimes translate as feeling anxious in harmonious relationships and more relaxed in the presence of drama. Another characteristic of anxiously attached people is that they struggle to bounce back after coming out of a stressful situation. Intense fears may linger in their bodies for weeks and months after the event took place. Nevertheless, this doesn't stop them from connecting with people, as they continue to crave safety and intimacy. Typical phrases that an ambivalent-insecure person might say when feeling stressed are "Why does this always happen?" or "I can't trust anyone."

Avoidant-insecure types have a very detached and clinical way of dealing with stress. On the surface, you would think that they are unaffected by what happens around them—but this is just a facade. Avoidant people feel the full effects of stress, similar to anyone else, but they choose to cope by minimizing or denying the impact. They act as though the stressful event is not a big deal and that perhaps everyone around them is overreacting to the stress. Deep down, they feel a heavy burden to solve the problem or maintain a strong self-image, in order to be seen as being in control.

When dealing with stress in interpersonal relationships, avoidant-insecure people are prone to shutting down, dismissing other people's feelings, or showing little empathy. While this may come across as callous, it is simply their way of self-regulating. Since the avoidant person has a lot of bottled emotions trapped inside of them, they are always fearful of being triggered and stepping out of character. Typical phrases they might say when feeling stressed are "I have this under control," or "Why are you making a big deal out of this?"

Disorganized-insecure types are more likely to feel confused than angry during times of stress. They might appear dazed, mentally dissociated, or withdrawn from what is happening around them. Due to their traumatic history, they have learned to "check out" or hide inside their shell whenever things feel too intense. They will also internalize the strong emotions they feel toward others or their life situation. Out of all the attachment types, these individuals are more prone to obsessions, like working a lot or eating excessively, or substance abuse problems, which occur as a result of not addressing their issues.

Key Takeaways

- Whether or not you are aware of it, your everyday interactions are influenced by your attachment style. This can stretch as far as to how you enjoy sexual intimacy.
- The benefit of learning more about your attachment style is that you can anticipate your responses to certain behaviors or events and mindfully adjust your reactions.

3

A Deep Dive Into Ambivalent-Insecure Attachment

"Imagine how much unnecessary anxiety we create when we live under the impression that our relationships should feel amazing all the time and that perfect happiness is an attainable goal!"

— SHEVA RAJEE

In this chapter you will learn:

- How ambivalence-insecure attachment develops
- Common signs of ambivalence-insecure attachment in relationships
- Some of the harmful habits that are practiced whenever attachment anxiety is triggered

How Does Ambivalent-Insecure Attachment Occur?

It's normal to be cautious when getting to know someone. After all, you aren't sure what type of person they are or how much you can trust them. However, these feelings subside the more information you learn about the individual and the deeper your connection grows.

The difference with people who have anxious attachment is that they never fully get comfortable around others, even when the connection has moved beyond surface level. The reason why we call this type of attachment "ambivalent" is because it is characterized by having "mixed feelings" or embracing contradictory ideas about others. In general, the contradiction occurs over feeling love and fear toward others—an experience that the anxious person had repeatedly when they were growing up.

An ambivalent-insecure attachment develops from early childhood when a child learns that they cannot rely on receiving consistent nurturing from their parents. Due to a variety of factors, their parents are unable to be emotionally available and responsive to their needs. This creates insecurity around the capacity to trust others and receive unconditional love. As adults, they can demonstrate a deep fear of rejection and abandonment in their relationships.

Many people assume that anxious children were never loved by their parents. However, this isn't always the case. It's possible that an anxious child was loved so much by their parents, to the extent of being overprotected. Perhaps you have encountered parents who are hypervigilant about their child's environment, where they go, what they eat, and who they hang around with.

Their desire to protect their child often causes them to invalidate the child's physical and emotional needs. This kind of "helicopter parenting" isn't necessarily inconsistent, but it can teach the child to associate closeness with controlling behavior. Later on in life, they might have mixed feelings about intimacy because they associate it with losing their sense of self.

Another example of loving children too much but invalidating their needs is a child raised by parents who are overly invested in their careers. They may undeniably love their child very much and view their work habits as a sacrifice to give their child the best possible life, yet being physically or emotionally absent creates an unstable and inconsistent connection with the child.

The role of caregiving may be assigned to nannies, schoolteachers, grandparents, or unfairly passed back to the child. This is made worse when nannies are constantly changed or the child is frequently moved from one school to another (or sent to boarding school at a young age). The child learns to fear making strong and lasting bonds because they can suddenly be taken away.

Signs of Ambivalent-Insecure Attachment

Researchers have found that not every anxious attachment looks the same. When looking for the signs of ambivalent-insecure attachment, we should remember that it exists on a spectrum. For instance, an individual can be ambivalent passive, ambivalent resistant, or lie somewhere in between those extremes.

Ambivalent resistant individuals tend to become visibly upset or withdrawn when they perceive a sense of rejection or abandonment. As children, they may have cried uncontrollably when being left by their parents. They may also engage in positive or negative attention-seeking behaviors to seek the approval of others or "win back" the affection of lovers. However, when others become emotionally available again, they may show their disapproval by being moody, withdrawing, or becoming angry.

On the other end of the spectrum, ambivalent passive individuals appear calm, cool, and collected on the surface, which might cause others to believe they are secure and unbothered about the perceived sense of rejection or abandonment. Instead of showing signs of anxiety, they typically internalize their emotions and downplay their own needs. Like other anxious people, they crave consistent and unconditional love but doubt that it is possible.

Both types of anxious people will, however, experience the same symptoms, which may include:

- **Clinginess:** An anxious person displays neediness in relationships, such as requiring constant reassurance about your partner's commitment, wanting constant communication with loved ones throughout the day (i.e. texting and calling religiously), and requiring regular support and check-ins.
- **Overwhelmed with emotional connections:** Ironically, those with anxious attachment can quickly become overwhelmed when relationships get too intense, as much as they are clingy. Since they are not used to being in consistent relationships where they are shown respect and love, they may develop a push and pull behavioral pattern.
- **Feel anxious in relationships:** A person with ambivalent-insecure attachment may be confident and secure in other areas

of their life but get easily triggered in close relationships. Small behaviors can raise fears of rejection and abandonment, such as a friend making an ambiguous comment.

- **Unpredictability:** Due to an anxious person's deep-seated trust issues, they find it difficult to see relationships lasting in the long-term. As a result, they don't do well in relationships with unpredictable or impulsive people because they trigger fears of abandonment.

- **Seeking validation:** An anxious person seeks constant reassurance from others to prove that their relationship is solid, that their connection is genuine, and that they are acceptable. Low self-esteem is one of the challenges that anxious people are faced with, regardless of how smart, attractive, or successful they are. When they are invalidated, they can become angry, withdrawn, or try even harder.

It may seem that anxious people are constantly looking for problems in a stable relationship, but what they are actually seeking is emotional safety. Remember, anxiety is the main driving force behind these unhealthy relational patterns, thus when an anxious person feels emotionally safe, they are able to manage their triggers.

It is therefore crucial for these individuals to learn about the different attachment styles and be mindful of the people they choose to connect with. Secure people bring out the best in them, while avoidant-insecure people bring out the worst in them. However, due to the behaviors of anxious people, they are more likely to attract avoidants, who confirm their fears of rejection and abandonment.

Harmful Habits to Avoid When Attachment Anxiety Is Triggered

The reason it can be so difficult to heal anxious attachment is due to the neurological changes made to the brain at an early age. Researchers have found that children with ambivalent-insecure attachment have a larger amygdala, which is the part of the brain that detects threats. As such, they tend to be more hyper-aware and prone to stress and anxiety than children with secure attachment. It also means that they can become easily triggered by threats that are unreal or blown out of proportion.

If you are prone to feeling anxious and vulnerable in relationships, it is important to carefully consider your actions. Of course, your first instinct may be to overreact and get as far away from the perceived danger. But what has been the outcome of taking this action over the years? Has it helped or harmed your relationships?

The following are a few more harmful habits that are likely to occur when your attachment anxiety is triggered. As you go through each habit, ask yourself: What have been the outcomes of taking these actions over the years?

Being Too Available and Consequently Abandoning Yourself

When you begin to feel insecure in a relationship, due to real or perceived signs of rejection or abandonment, you may start to become increasingly needy and self-sacrificing. Investing so much energy in maintaining the relationship means less time spent on taking care of yourself. Signs that you are abandoning yourself include double-texting or being the one to always initiate conversations, stalking the person on social media, or dedicating all of your weekends to being with them.

Compromising Your Beliefs and Values to Make the Other Person Happy

Have you ever found yourself silently cringing when one of your values is violated, but you pretend as though it isn't such a big deal because you don't want to upset the other person? This pattern tends to show up in codependent relationships, where you merge identities and adopt the same values and interests as your partner. In the long run, this can lead to the loss of individuality and weak boundaries.

Self-Sabotage Instead of Self-Awareness

In many cases, when you feel anxious in relationships, old childhood trauma is triggered. In that moment, you can "black out" and time travel back to the past. How you react is dependent on how you reacted as a child whenever you felt neglected. For instance, you might withdraw without saying a word to your friend or partner because that is how you coped with these strong feelings when you were younger. You may also turn to other forms of self-sabotage that you picked up later in life, such as binge drinking, starting an affair, self-harm, or working extreme hours.

Negative Self-Talk

You may have a habit of internalizing your hurt feelings and subsequently blaming yourself for the inconsistencies in a relationship. For example, if you don't hear back from a colleague after a certain number of days, you might assume that you have offended them. The pattern of self-blame leads to negative self-talk, where you constantly criticize yourself for not living up to others' standards or not being able to maintain a relationship. Due to the negative self-talk, you may even fear entering new relationships because of not wanting to replay the negative thoughts in your mind.

Fantasizing About Being Saved

The inconsistencies in love that you experienced early in life may create fantasies about finding true love or being rescued by someone who understands and accepts you. These fantasies aren't necessarily bad, as long as they aren't projected onto people. For example, projecting the fantasy of a soulmate onto a new romantic partner can lead to neediness and people-pleasing behavior. In exchange for your devotion, you expect them to live up to your dream of an ideal partner. When they don't live up to this fantasy—and instead show you that they are only human—you can feel a sense of betrayal and become distrustful of them.

Most of the time, you may not be aware of these habits. But if you take the time to reflect on your current or past relationship patterns, you will see the same triggers and reactions playing out. It's important not to judge yourself for reacting unfavorably when you are triggered, but instead seek to learn more about what unmet needs are being revealed in those moments.

Key Takeaways

- Ambivalent-insecure attachment style develops as a result of inconsistent parenting. A child learns very early on that they cannot trust their parents to be emotionally available and responsive all of the time.

- There are two ways ambivalent-insecure attachment can manifest: an individual can either be ambivalent resistant (lashing out when their needs aren't met) or ambivalent passive (suppressing unmet needs and pretending as though they are unaffected).
- Common signs of an anxious attachment in relationships include clinginess, seeking validation, feeling anxious with unpredictability, and pushing people away when the emotional connection starts to deepen.
- Since anxiety is one of the main markers of anxious attachment, it is important to recognize how you react whenever your anxiety is triggered. Being aware of your reactions can help you find alternative coping strategies that allow you to manage anxiety in more positive ways.

II

Confronting Anxious Attachment

4

Different Ways to Regulate Your Nervous System

"When you are feeling emotional, it is helpful to remind yourself, as a self-regulating measure, 'The past is not here. This is the present."

— SHELLEY KLAMMER

In this chapter you will learn:

- How the stress response is triggered in the brain and physiological signs to look out for
- Different relaxation techniques to regulate your nervous system and return to a calm and balanced state of mind
- How to create your own stress management toolkit, including a crisis management plan and weekly relaxation practice

Recognizing When You Are Triggered

When your sense of security is threatened in a relationship, for whatever possible reason, you become triggered. The word "trigger" is popular in psychology and pop culture, and it seeks to explain an experience where an individual has a strong emotional reaction to something or someone that reminds them of a past traumatic event.

Author of *It's Not Always Depression*, Hilary Jacobs Hendel mentions how triggers activate the "three brains," namely the thinking, emotional, and body brain (Hendel, 2018). When you are triggered, the three brains respond as follows:

- The thinking brain says, "This situation looks awfully familiar to what I have experienced before."
- The emotional brain says, "I feel anxious, therefore I must be in trouble!"
- The body brain says, "My heart is racing faster, I find it difficult to breathe. Run as fast as you can from this situation!"

None of the three brains take a moment to understand what is actually happening in the present moment or choose to see the situation from a fresh perspective. They react based on existing patterns of thinking and behavior.

In other words, if you have always withdrawn yourself from others when you sense rejection, your three brains will encourage you to follow the same behavior. This reveals something very important about triggers: They exist because of unresolved past trauma.

Due to the fact that you are unconsciously carrying emotional wounds from stressful or abusive past relationships, everyday encounters with people make you feel vulnerable. You are more likely to be triggered by a text, call, or snarky remark—even when these events aren't offensive—because of the trauma-based information that informs your thoughts, emotions, and behaviors.

Understanding your anxious attachment style can come in handy when seeking to learn more about your relationship triggers. It enables you to look at the different kinds of interactions or experiences that bring up feelings of anxiety. For instance, you might discover that your attachment anxiety is caused by external and internal relationship triggers.

External relationship triggers arise from your interpersonal relationships with close friends and family, coworkers, romantic partners, and other members of your community. You might be triggered by the words, phrases, tones of voice, body gestures, facial expressions, or attitudes displayed by others. For example, a friend who has the tendency of not checking up on you can be a source of trigger, so can a romantic partner who shows a lack of empathy.

What's worth remembering about external relationship triggers is that you cannot blame another individual for the emotional distress you experience. The only thing you can hold them accountable for are their actions or misjudgments, but the strong reaction that develops inside of you has more to do with your attachment issues than the individual's behavior. This is why when you express feeling hurt by someone's actions, you are advised to use "I" statements to show ownership of your emotional experience.

Another type of trigger you might experience are internal relationship triggers. These tend to arise from within and are based on troublesome thoughts or unpleasant emotions. Examples include negative self-talk, limiting self-beliefs, anxiety, loneliness, and depression. When you experience a thought or emotion that reminds you of a time when you were most vulnerable, full of self-doubt or anger, or felt confused, your brain assumes that the same incident is taking place again and you react with the same coping mechanisms as before.

Your reactions may be alarming to those around you because they don't understand how the current situation justifies the extreme emotional reaction. They may see your behavior as being exaggerated, dramatic, or impulsive because it doesn't match reality. The truth of the matter is that they are correct but that doesn't mean what you are experiencing isn't valid. If they aren't familiar with your attachment style, they won't be able to empathize with your behaviors and see that you have mentally regressed to the little boy or girl who felt anxious and unsafe.

Both external and internal triggers will continue to feature in your life until you get behind them and heal the parts of you that are still wounded. Nevertheless, recognizing triggers is winning half of the battle. When you are aware of your reactions to various triggering situations, you have the power to choose a favorable response.

How to Calm Your Nervous System

When your attachment anxiety is triggered, you can feel lost and helpless. The initial thought might be "Here we go again!" before a wave of anxiety floods your body. The first step of healing from anxious attachment is acknowledging that relationships are stressful for you. As much as you would like to open up to others and sustain long-term mutually beneficial relationships, this won't be easy for you.

Acknowledging that you find relationships stressful helps you antic-ipate flare ups of anxiety in everyday encounters, rather than being shocked by them. You anticipate that your brain will ring alarm bells for trivial mistakes that others make, almost like a whining child who cries out when feeling the slightest discomfort. Try not to judge yourself for being so sensitive to offense or sudden changes in relationships; simply acknowledge that due to your upbringing, you are constantly on high alert.

Besides acknowledgment, another important step to take is to learn about the natural stress response and the process that is carried out whenever your brain senses potential threats. The following is a brief summary of the interaction between the brain, nervous system, and the rest of your body. Note that this interaction happens within seconds, and you won't always be aware of it.

- Your eyes or ears send information to a part of your brain known as the amygdala. The amygdala is responsible for emotionally pro-cessing the information, such as interpreting whether a situation is safe or unsafe.
- When danger is perceived, the amygdala sends a distress signal to another part of your brain known as the hypothalamus. The hypothalamus is responsible for ringing the alarm bells and notify-ing the rest of the body of a possible threat. This communication happens through the autonomic nervous system.
- The autonomic nervous system controls a host of body functions, like breathing, heart rate, and blood pressure. Since its job is so large, it is divided into two parts: the sympathetic and parasympathetic nervous system.
- The sympathetic nervous system sends stress signals throughout the body and activates the fight-flight-freeze response. When it

45

is engaged, you may notice your heart rate accelerating, breath shortening, blood pressure rising, etc.

- The parasympathetic nervous system is responsible for regulating and reducing stress signals until the body returns to a resting state. It is usually engaged after the perceived threat is removed, but if you are familiar with relaxation techniques, you can switch it on.

What is "natural" for your brain and body when you experience attachment anxiety is to send distress signals to the sympathetic nervous system and begin a chain of physiological reactions to stress. What is less common is becoming aware of what is happening and immediately activating the parasympathetic nervous system, so you can regulate the stress response and remain grounded.

There are a number of different relaxation techniques that you can turn to whenever you sense a trigger or notice physiological signs of being stressed. Here are just a few of these techniques, which you can practice in the comfort of your home. After going through the techniques, create your own stress management toolkit, including a crisis management plan and weekly relaxation practice (more instructions to follow).

Breathing Exercises

"Just breathe" sounds like a straightforward instruction, but when you are anxious and your heart rate and breathing are irregular, it can be difficult to remember how to "just breathe."

Research has shown that breathing not only sustains life but can also activate your parasympathetic nervous system, which sends signals to your brain that the perceived threat no longer exists (Sinclair, 2021). Taking slower and deeper breaths also allows more oxygen to the brain, which can leave you feeling calm.

So, how do you just breathe? One of the most common and effective breathing exercises taught in therapy is diaphragmatic breathing, or belly breathing. The aim is to lengthen each breath as much as possible and slowly release.

Patients are usually told to direct their breaths to their stomachs, rather than staying at the chest area, to ensure they take fuller breaths. Follow these steps to practice diaphragmatic breathing:

1. Lie down on a bed with your face looking toward the ceiling and legs slightly apart. Take a few normal breaths to get comfortable in this position.
2. Place your left hand on your chest and your right hand on your belly. For the rest of the exercise, ensure that your left hand remains completely still. Only your right hand should move up and down.
3. When you are ready, inhale slowly through your nose and stretch your breath until it reaches your belly. A good way to tell if you are doing the movement correctly is to watch your stomach rise.
4. Hold the breath for a brief moment, then slowly exhale out of your mouth, until there is no more air left inside of you. Once again, you will know that you are doing the movement correctly by watching your stomach fall back down.
5. Continue taking slow and full breaths for another five minutes.

Diaphragmatic breathing is not the only exercise that can help you regulate your breathing. Another effective exercise is known as box breathing. The aim of box breathing is to teach you how to take control of your breathing and gradually bring your heart and breathing rate back to a resting state. The following are the instructions to perform box breathing:

1. Inhale through your nose for five slow and consistent counts.
2. Hold your breath for another five slow and consistent counts.
3. Exhale out of your mouth for five slow and consistent counts.
4. Hold your breath for another five slow and consistent counts.
5. If five counts is uncomfortable for you, feel free to drop the count to four or three.
6. Continue practicing this breathing pattern multiple times.

The magic of breathing exercises is how they simultaneously relax the mind and body. The final breathing exercise that will be presented to you seeks to strengthen the mind-body connection by making mental suggestions. It is known as focused breathing.

The aim of focused breathing is to think of a positive word, mental or emotional state, or mantra that you can bring to mind whenever you inhale. Imagine that you were filling your body with an abundance of this particular experience. As you exhale, imagine that you are ridding your body of the opposite, negative experience that you may be exposed to.

For example, after having a call with your parent, you feel a sudden emergence of frustration. This would be the negative experience you want to get rid of. But what could be the positive experience you desire in its place? Maybe you would like to feel peace whenever you speak to your parent, or maybe you need a mantra that reminds you that you cannot change or control other people.

The next step is to close your eyes, take a deep breath in, and imagine you were taking in an abundance of peace. Hold your breath for a brief moment, then as you exhale, imagine you were releasing the pent up frustration. Continue doing this until you feel a noticeable difference in your mood.

Mindfulness Exercises

Mindfulness is a relaxation technique that is borrowed and has been adapted from the Buddhist tradition. Being mindful involves focusing on present experiences, whether it be sounds, sights, smells, thoughts, or feelings.

The reason mindfulness is so effective in calming the nervous system is due to how it reduces mind wandering. Remember, attachment anxiety is triggered by the recollection of past traumatic experiences in intimate relationships.

When you are able to refocus on the present moment, you will notice that the fears of rejection or abandonment become less intense or believable. Moreover, you are able to correctly perceive what is taking place, without mentally regressing to the past.

There are many different kinds of mindfulness exercises you can practice embracing the present moment. One of them is to complete a simple mindfulness meditation.

With your eyes closed, the aim is to acknowledge thoughts passing through your mind, without unpacking them or forming opinions about them. After acknowledging each thought, you take a deep breath and let it go. You can follow this script to complete a mindfulness meditation:

Find a quiet spot at home or in the office. Put your phone on silent and set a timer for 5 minutes. Get yourself in a comfortable position where your body is relaxed and muscles disengaged. Close your eyes and complete a short box breathing exercise.

When you are ready, take a deep breath and listen for any incoming thoughts. Your mind may be buzzing with thoughts like a busy highway, or it may be calm like a suburban street on a Sunday afternoon. Take a few moments to observe the activity without participating in it.

Categorize each thought by its size. Notice how many large, medium, and small thoughts are circulating in your mind. Choose whichever thoughts you want to acknowledge. Perhaps during this session, you only want to acknowledge small thoughts, but in another session you may be willing to acknowledge larger thoughts.

Once you have chosen the category of thoughts to acknowledge, focus on a single thought within that category. Make this thought the sole focus of your mind. Be careful not to identify with or attach yourself to the thought. Just look at it, accept the message it has to share with you, then let it go.

For example, a fear-based thought may want to alert you about somebody's unfavorable behavior. Acknowledge and accept the message, then let the thought go. Continue doing this until there are no more thoughts left in that specific category or until the timer goes off.

Another great mindfulness exercise is the body scan. This is an awareness exercise that can improve your sensory perceptiveness, which is the ability to recognize the different sensations you are feeling in your body.

This kind of awareness can help you detect the physical signs of stress or emotional triggers before they get bigger and become overwhelming.

The traditional way of completing a body scan requires you to lie down on a bed (similar position as diaphragmatic breathing) and take your time moving from one muscle group to the next, looking for any physical or emotional discomfort.

To identify emotional discomfort, it might help to close your eyes and visualize the specific muscle group in your mind and see if there are any thoughts or emotions that arise.

An alternative way to practice the body scan is to match a body sensation with a feeling. For this, you don't need to lie down, but the exercise works best when you are resting. Take your right hand and place it on an area of your body where you sense physical or emotional discomfort. Thereafter, mention what you are sensing and what feeling it brings up.

For example, you may sense physical discomfort around your chest area. You can proceed by taking your right hand and placing it on your chest. Then you can say a simple phrase like "My chest is tight. I feel anxious."

This level of awareness can immediately bring some sort of relief because you are able to gain control of your experience and choose how to react moving forward.

Grounding Exercises

Grounding is an effective relaxation technique, especially for countering anxiety and panic attacks. The aim of grounding is to "connect to earth" or snap back to reality.

Grounding exercises put the power back in your hands by giving you control of the moment. You are able to disengage from negative self-talk or overthinking, empty your mind, and interact with your surroundings.

Some people refer to grounding exercises as positive distractions, and this is true. Essentially, you are distracting yourself from the ongoing chitter-chatter in the mind by focusing on something emotionally neutral, like counting the objects in a room. This can give your body enough time to de-stress and return to a normal resting state.

There are various types of grounding exercises you can experiment with. All of them seek to reconnect you with your surroundings. The first is known as the "5-4-3-2-1 exercise." The challenge is to activate your five senses, scan your environment, and identify:

- 5 things you can see with your eyes
- 4 things you can smell with your nose
- 3 things you can touch with your hands
- 2 things you can hear with your ears
- 1 thing you can taste with your tongue

If you like, you can walk around the room and physically point or grab the items. Adding some movement to the exercise further brings you into the present moment.

Another great grounding exercise is to deliberately adjust your body temperature by exposing yourself to colder temperatures. This triggers a shock in your body and activates the parasympathetic nervous system. Simple ways to do this are running your hands under cold tap water, taking a cold shower or swim, suckling on an ice cube, or placing a cold cloth on your forehead.

Furthermore, you can ground yourself by completing a reorienting exercise. This involves reminding yourself, out loud, what date it is, where you are, what is taking place, etc. For example, when you are triggered at the office you can say to yourself:

"My name is Ashley. I am 32 years old. The date today is May 3rd. The year is 2023. The time is 12 noon. I am in the office boardroom trying to calm myself down. In a few minutes I will stand up and take my lunch. I am having a sandwich and soda for lunch."

Reorienting yourself prevents mental regression, which is common when your attachment anxiety is triggered. It sends a message to your brain that you are not having the same childhood experience. You are older now, in a different place, having a completely new experience.

Examples of a few more positive distractions to ground yourself include:

- Count from 0 to 10 then from 10 to 0, slowly. If your mind wanders, start the counting again.
- Count how many letters are in the phrase "I am safe and in control," or any other phrase you can think of.
- Try to recall whose birthday is this month. Or whose birthday is coming up. What date is their birthday?

- Recite the lyrics to your favorite positive song.
- Recite the alphabet backward.
- Recall the recipe to make your favorite meal.
- Call a friend who puts a smile on your face.
- Read a page from a daily devotional.
- Say a silent prayer.
- Complete 10 jumping jacks and 10 squats.

Visualization Exercises

Visualization is about seeing things in your mind that haven't yet materialized. This requires tapping into your imagination and envisioning a future-based outcome. Since the brain doesn't understand the concept of time (i.e. past, present, future), it assumes that what you are visualizing is taking place in the present moment.

In therapy, visualization exercises are used to make positive mental suggestions that, with enough repetition, can positively affect your mood and overall sense of well-being. When you sense a trigger coming along, for example, you can close your eyes and visualize a peaceful setting. Not only can this serve as a positive distraction, but it can also suggest to your brain that you are safe and calm.

There are some who discount visualization exercises, citing that it is merely "wishful thinking." But study the lives of top-performing athletes or successful entrepreneurs, and you will notice how mental rehearsals (i.e. visualization) are an important part of planning, decision-making, and executing goals.

There are many ways to practice visualization; some are conventional, and others will push you outside of your comfort zone. A conventional visualization exercise is creating a vision or mood board, which is a tool used to constantly remind you of the life or relationship goals you are striving for.

All you need to create a vision or mood board is a large piece of cardboard paper, a few magazine images and word cut outs, and craft supplies. If you wish to create a digital board, you can download an app like Corkulous or Dream Vision Board App. Place your board somewhere accessible so that you can look at it on a regular basis.

Another conventional exercise is to create index cards. These cards also serve as a positive reminder of your goals. The aim is to read over your cards once a day, preferably in the morning, or whenever you are feeling overwhelmed.

On about 10–20 flashcards, write down goals for your relationships. You can include goals like being a good listener, holding emotional space for someone, or taking deep breaths when feeling attacked. Under each goal, write a short description of what that might look like in real life. Every day, shuffle your cards and go through as many as you like. Pause after reading each goal and reflect on the progress you are making in that area.

Now for some unconventional visualization exercises! You have probably heard of positive affirmations before but perhaps haven't practiced them because you don't like the sound of your voice or maybe don't think they work.

Positive affirmations are affirmative statements that suggest certain thoughts and feelings to the subconscious mind. Since the work happens on a subconscious level, you might assume the statements aren't working. But the truth is that each time you recite affirmative statements to yourself, you are dismantling old thinking patterns and building new ones.

Whether you repeat the positive affirmations in front of a mirror or on the car ride to work, what matters is that you say them out loud. Hearing yourself speak positively is part of the reprogramming. Essentially, you are convincing your brain to adopt a positive truth.

The basic structure of a positive affirmation is to start with "I" and structure the sentence in present tense, as though what you are affirming about yourself is already happening. For example, you might say

- I show up as my authentic self in relationships.
- I am an asset to my friends and family.
- I am open to accepting people who are different from me.
- I am patient with myself and others.
- I am calm during conflict.

What makes positive affirmations effective is personalizing them for the specific areas of your relationship you struggle with, such as trusting others, feeling relaxed, or expressing your feelings. Your affirmations need to make sense to you and target your anxiety triggers.

Another unconventional visualization exercise is exposing yourself to the desired experiences you hope to achieve. In practical terms, getting exposure requires you to step outside of your comfort zone and immerse yourself in a new environment.

For example, if you would like to adopt a secure attachment in your romantic relationship, getting exposure would entail hanging around couples who have a secure attachment or watching videos of people talking about secure attachment.

This could also mean avoiding online content or couples that promote or exhibit insecure attachments or unhealthy patterns of behavior. The more you saturate your world with people or content that encourage strictly secure attachment, the more "normal" it will be for you to behave in secure ways in your romantic relationship.

Stress Management Toolkit

Now that you have gone through the different types of relaxation exercises to regulate your nervous system, it is time to put together your own stress management toolkit. The toolkit will consist of your selection of exercises to practice whenever you are feeling overwhelmed.

To create your toolkit, start by writing down a list of common anxiety triggers you experience in everyday life. For example, a trigger at home might be receiving the silent treatment from your partner and a trigger at work might be being spoken to harshly by your boss.

For each trigger, find at least one relaxation exercise you can practice whenever it arises. Write them down on the lines provided.

Next, think about the situations that you fear most in relationships, such as being rejected, criticized, verbally attacked, or alienated by your group of friends. Write them down.

For each situation, find at least one relaxation exercise that can help you cope whenever the fear is triggered. For example, what can you do when you start to feel alienated or pushed out of your friendship group? Note that the fear can be triggered even when there isn't a real threat.

Part of managing stress involves making relaxation a daily practice. Think about the types of stressors you deal with on a daily basis, such as parenting, dealing with a toxic boss, taking care of an ill parent, etc.

Create a daily relaxation routine, either morning or evening routine, which can help to alleviate stress and anxiety. Your routine should have a minimum of three exercises. Feel free to include other calming exercises that were not included in this chapter.

Commit to your morning or evening relaxation routine for three consecutive days and journal about your experience.

Key Takeaways

- When the brain detects a perceived threat, it sends warning signals to the autonomic nervous system, which activates the sympathetic nervous system. This leads to a chain of physiological changes to the body, including increased heart and breathing rate.
- Eventually, when the threat subsides, the parasympathetic nervous system will be activated, which brings the heart and breathing rate back to normal and induces a state of calm.
- When you understand how the nervous system works, you can manage the stress response and control your mental and physical state. The relaxation exercises mentioned in this chapter are effective in reversing the effects of stress and calming the mind and body. Daily practice of these exercises can help you respond to signs of stress from the onset and maintain a sense of balance.

5

Prepare for a Paradigm Shift

"We speak about losing our minds as if it is a bad thing. I say, lose your mind. Do it purposefully. Find out who you really are beyond your thoughts and beliefs. Lose your mind, find your soul."

— VIRONIKA TUGALEVA

In this chapter you will learn:

- The nature of limiting beliefs and how to tell when you are ready to let them go
- The five steps to complete the CBT cognitive restructuring technique and replace limiting beliefs

Outgrowing Your Attachment Style

One of the things worth emphasizing time again is the importance of not judging yourself for having developed anxious attachment.

Judgment implies that how you have approached relationships for the past decades has been wrong, shameful, or unacceptable. However, the story around how you developed your anxious attachment is more complicated than that.

Your attachment style developed out of survival, not a deliberate choice. If you could have chosen, you would have gone with a secure attachment. After all, which child doesn't crave unconditional love and acceptance from their parents? But unfortunately, due to various life circumstances, your parents weren't emotionally available for you, and you were left with no other choice than to adapt and find ways to cope.

Back when you were a child, withdrawing to your room, faking happiness, or seeking approval from others was what worked. Of course, in hindsight, you can see how harmful these coping strategies were (and continue to be) but in your younger years they created a sense of safety.

Now that you are much older, and maybe have kids of your own, you desire to respond to your attachment anxiety differently-using coping strategies that don't sabotage your relationships.

Everybody reaches a stage in their lives where they feel unsatisfied with their current belief system and wish to update how they perceive the world and others. This drive for change can be triggered by personal growth, forgiving a wrongdoer (or receiving an apology from a wrongdoer), making positive new connections, or having a life-altering spiritual experience.

Due to the changes in your life, you start to ask questions about your childhood, relationships with your parents, or about your personality traits. Living under the old belief system, carrying out the old routines, or maintaining dysfunctional relationships becomes increasingly uncomfortable.

If you are at this stage, it is no coincidence that you are reading a book about how to overcome anxious attachment. In your attempts to understand yourself better, you have often wondered why relationships are so stressful and difficult for you.

In many healing journeys, the first step is always acknowledgment. Acknowledging what is not working out creates enough openness to dig deeper and find relief for your pain. Now that you are beginning to acknowledge that your anxious attachment isn't bringing fulfillment in your relationships, you can start to look deeper and understand the beliefs that are holding you back.

Limiting Beliefs That Sabotage Your Relationships

There is a quote by Deepak Chopra that says, "The less you open your heart to others, the more your heart suffers" (Vishnu, 2015). Some might challenge this argument and state the opposite, that the less you open your heart, the less suffering you will experience.

You can test this second argument by reflecting back on your life. Grab a pen and two sheets of paper and write two diary entries as though you had time traveled to two periods of your life: A period when your heart was open and you were able to give and receive love, and a period when your heart was closed and you could not give or receive love. Your diary entry can include typical thoughts, emotions, beliefs, and behaviors you exhibited during both periods.

Now that you have completed the exercise, what can you say about Chopra's quote? Would you side with him and agree that closing your heart brings on suffering or would you say that closing your heart prevents suffering?

Exercises like these, often referred to as cognitive restructuring or reappraisal, are extremely important when you are gearing toward making lifestyle changes. They allow you to pause, think about your beliefs, weigh the pros and cons, and arrive at your own conclusions about whether they are helpful or harmful to your understanding of people and life in general.

When you were a child, you didn't have the psychological tools to critically think about and challenge your beliefs. You simply saw behavior taking place around you and came up with a simple explanation of what was happening. For example, a little child often cries when their parents drop them off at school because in their minds they believe that is the last time they will see their parents.

Of course, this isn't what is actually taking place because within a few hours, their parents will return to pick them up. But in the absence of reflecting and challenging their belief, they are left with a painful wound of separation. Now imagine that the same child faced multiple traumas during their childhood, which caused them to come up with multiple beliefs that were not "fact-checked" or challenged. How differently might they perceive the world around them due to holding onto these beliefs?

Unchecked and unchallenged beliefs continue with you into adulthood and affect your relationships in many ways, such as triggering attachment anxiety. The earlier you identify them and go through the process of cognitive restructuring or reappraisal, the sooner you can decide to keep or discard them.

Here are examples of limiting beliefs that are common among people with anxious attachment:

- **"I'm broken."**

In the previous chapter we spoke about the power of positive affirmations and how they seek to reprogram subconscious thought patterns. The belief "I'm broken" is a negative affirmation that confirms a feeling or state of brokenness.

When you repeatedly tell yourself that something is wrong with you, you subconsciously validate dysfunctional patterns of behavior. After all, if something is truly wrong with you, then it makes sense why you cannot maintain healthy and mutually beneficial relationships, right?

You might be saying to yourself, "Well, what if I actually feel broken, is it so wrong to believe that?" The answer is no, it is not wrong to feel broken-what's wrong is identifying with brokenness. There is a difference between saying "I feel broken" and "I am broken." The latter makes it more difficult to challenge the belief because that is who you are.

- **"No one will ever love me again."**

It is common when coming out of a good relationship to believe that you won't ever find another partner who can love you the same. This belief only sounds true because you can only compare your ex-partner to past partners. But since you cannot travel to the future, there is no way of knowing if your previous good relationship was indeed your last.

What's also worth noting about this belief is the extreme exaggeration, also known as catastrophizing. This is a harmful thinking habit that causes you to make the worst possible conclusion, which most times doesn't match reality. There are so many logical errors with the belief that it cannot be conceivably true. Nonetheless, your mind is inclined to believe that it's true because of the constant reinforcement.

- **"I don't bring any value to relationships."**

One of the side effects of having low self-esteem is thinking that there is nothing good that you have to offer others. Overtime, this belief becomes a self-fulfilling prophecy because if you don't believe you have anything worthwhile to share, you are less likely to reveal your strengths in relationships. You won't see the point of trying to get to know people, revealing your nurturing side, or serving others.

Furthermore, when people believe they bring no value, many times they are referring to extrinsic value, which is the value given to someone by society based on status, power, acceptable standards (i.e. beauty), or materialistic possession (i.e. how much money you have).

Evaluating your worth based on extrinsic value is like gambling with your self-esteem. For example, when you're in a committed relationship, you feel valuable, but the moment you break up, you feel worthless because singleness is looked down upon. Perhaps when you have a lot of disposable money to spend on your partner, you feel valuable, but the moment you can't afford to shower them with gifts, you feel worthless because of the pressure to protect and provide (often experienced by men in the dating world).

Instead it is better to evaluate your sense of self-worth based on intrinsic value, which is the value you determine for yourself based on unique character traits, skills and talents, personal achievements, and the positive impact you make in the lives of others. Intrinsic value doesn't rise or drop when your external circumstances change. It remains consistent whether you've reached a successful point in your life or are still working toward it.

Moreover, your intrinsic value isn't decreased when others fail to recognize your strengths and uniqueness. This can also free you from constantly seeking validation from others or blaming yourself for others' actions.

- **"Knowing myself, I'll find a way to sabotage this new relationship."**

Another self-fulfilling prophecy is believing that what has happened in the past will happen again.

There is some level of truth to this belief but only in certain contexts. For example, the past repeats itself if the same patterns are followed. If your pattern is to pull back whenever a relationship starts to get intense, then that is what will continue to happen. The past will also repeat itself when the environment stays the same. For example, if you continue to surround yourself or maintain relationships that are invalidating, lack boundaries, and fail to respond to your needs, then there isn't much fulfillment you can expect to receive from your relationships.

Take the time to think about the reasons you sabotage relationships.

What informs that behavior? Is there a harmful pattern that you continue to follow, or are you part of an unsupportive and unhealthy environment? Take accountability where it is due and make the necessary changes.

- **"It's dangerous to be vulnerable."**

Children who develop anxious attachment learn not to trust those closest to them. Later on in life, they may struggle to be vulnerable with others because of deep trust issues.

As a child, it might have felt safest to shut down your emotions and put on a tough exterior, but that could've also led to feelings of loneliness and depression. The truth is vulnerability isn't dangerous. It is the gateway to unconditional love and intimacy. Only by choosing to be vulnerable can a person experience what it means to be known and accepted by someone else.

The danger is opening up to the wrong people who don't have your best interests at heart. Having core values and knowing your personal boundaries can help you keep the wrong people at a distance, while remaining open to those who genuinely care about you.

Making a Paradigm Shift

A paradigm shift is a term that was coined by physicist Thomas Kuhn and explained in his book *The Structure of Scientific Revolutions* (MasterClass, 2022). From a scientific point of view, a paradigm shift refers to a change that occurs when a scientific activity contradicts previous belief that experts found to be indisputable. As a result, a new "paradigm" or belief replaces the old.

In modern psychology, a paradigm shift can refer to the process of challenging existing beliefs that previously seemed indisputable and replacing them with newer beliefs that match your current worldview. These shifts don't happen regularly since they involve questioning the status quo of your life. Even then, it is still difficult to confront beliefs that have played a major role in how you see yourself and interact with others.

Nonetheless, making a paradigm shift can be liberating. The best way to explain the benefit of a paradigm shift is making an analogy with tight jeans. Have you ever had a favorite pair of jeans that became too tight after years? At some point, those tight jeans fit you like a glove, but with time—and generous helpings of candy and desserts—they become uncomfortable to wear.

From the outside, nobody knew how pressed you felt in those jeans because they looked perfectly normal, but since you were aware of the body changes that had taken place and how the jeans were supposed to feel, you preferred to end your misery and buy a new pair.

When current beliefs become limiting, they start to feel constricting and uncomfortable. In the past you may have been able to justify the beliefs and even support why you felt that way, but with time and change that is no longer how you feel. Making a paradigm shift can help you rethink ideas, thoughts, and memories that have gone unchallenged for many years. Doing this allows you to audit your belief system and replace those beliefs that are no longer appropriate or aligned to your evolved worldview.

Signs You Are Ready for a Paradigm Shift

As you grow and encounter new experiences, your mind expands with new information. You can now look at the same life circumstances from multiple perspectives and challenge ideas that you previously didn't have the knowledge to oppose.

There are a few signs you can look out for that show you are ready for a paradigm shift. These include:

1. You feel disconnected from your current norms and routines.
     The first sign that you are ready for a paradigm shift is that you no longer find satisfaction in the everyday norms and routines. Life may start to feel like a drag, and you don't have the same energy and passion for your work, health, and relationships.

2. You feel a void that cannot be filled.
     It is also common to sense an inner void or emptiness that doesn't seem to go away, regardless of how you might fill it. Another way of saying this is that you feel stuck and can't move your life forward. Deep down, you know that something is wrong but don't exactly know what the issue might be.

3. You expect more from your relationships.
     You are ready for a paradigm shift when you start to expect more from your relationships. Unpleasant behaviors that you previously allowed become increasingly intolerable for you. You may even be more aware of boundary violations than you were before, which can lead to avoidant behaviors or confrontations.

4. You start to question your past narratives.

When you are ready for a paradigm shift, your past becomes a fascination or obsession. You start to ask yourself questions about the way you were raised, the traumas you experienced, and why things had to turn out the way they did. The big questions are about getting as close as possible to understanding the truth about your life and breaking free from disempowering ideas and beliefs.

5. Your outlook on the world is changing.

Life looks different when you are in survival mode compared to when you are venturing on a journey of healing. The difference is the way in which you perceive the world. When you are about to embark on a paradigm shift, you may look at the world with openness and greater self-awareness. Instead of maintaining high walls that prevent others from getting close, you approach new experiences with curiosity.

Five Steps to Challenge and Replace Limiting Beliefs

If you are ready for a paradigm shift and can attest to experiencing one or more of the signs mentioned in the previous section, then you can proceed by embarking on the process of cognitive restructuring. As mentioned earlier, cognitive restructuring is a psychological technique based on the principles of cognitive behavioral therapy (CBT), which can help you challenge and replace limiting beliefs.

The aim of cognitive restructuring is to create enough distance between you and your thoughts, emotions, and beliefs, so that you can examine them objectively. Therefore, as you follow the five steps of cognitive restructuring outlined next, avoid identifying with your thoughts, emotions, and beliefs. Imagine that you were an observer looking into your situation and assessing it from an unbiased viewpoint.

71

Step 1: Describe the Situation

In general, beliefs aren't triggered out of nowhere. There is usually a situation in question that triggers a particular limiting belief. For the purpose of this exercise, recall a recent relationship situation that triggered attachment anxiety. It could have been an altercation with a coworker, misunderstanding with your partner, or actions taken by your family members, etc.

In the space provided, describe what happened. Mention the actions that were taken by all parties involved. Avoid making any assumptions.

_____

_____

_____

_____

Step 2: Express How You Felt

Now that the details are out of the way, share your emotional experience. Describe how you felt before, during, and after the situation. Strictly mention your own emotional experience and how you were impacted. Use "I" statements to show ownership of your emotions. For example, "I felt disrespected because he refused to listen to me."

_____

_____

_____

_____

Step 3: Identify Your Limiting Beliefs

In CBT, patients learn that their emotions, thoughts, and behaviors are related. For instance, feeling an intense emotion can trigger an unwanted thought or belief, which causes you to take certain actions or reinforce behavioral patterns.

Therefore, in this step, identify the limiting beliefs that flooded your mind while you were processing your emotions. For example, if you were anxious, what bad thing did you expect to happen? Or if you felt disrespected, how did you see yourself in that moment? Look for the "negative meaning" that you ascribed to the situation taking place.

Step 4: Challenge Your Limiting Beliefs

This step is the most critical because it is when the paradigm shift occurs. For all this time, you have allowed the limiting beliefs to go unchecked and unchallenged. It may not have been an issue for you until now. Without being biased, you have an opportunity to look at the belief from all angles, weigh the pros and cons, and assess whether you believe it to be true.

The goal of challenging your limiting beliefs isn't to assume that they are wrong simply because they sound negative. You must provide your brain with enough substantial proof (e.g. factual evidence) to show that your belief is inaccurate. With enough evidence, it will be easier to ignore the belief whenever it appears in your mind or to replace it with a more convincing one.

There are different ways to challenge beliefs. The first is to write down a list of reasons why you feel that way. Afterward, go through each reason and write down whether it is a fact or opinion. Count how many of the reasons are facts versus opinions. If there are more facts than opinions, it means that there is substantial evidence to prove the belief is true. However, if many of the reasons are opinions, then the belief needs to undergo further questioning.

Another way is to reflect on where the belief originated. Try to recall the earliest memory of embracing the belief. How old were you? What was happening? How did you feel at the time? Some beliefs emerge out of childhood trauma and pain. During this time, they seem helpful because they bring instant comfort or shed light on a situation. But overtime, they can be limiting and cause you to adopt an inaccurate understanding of what actually happened.

You might also find that some limiting beliefs were borrowed from other people. For example, if you were raised by a parent who had low self-esteem, you might have adopted similar beliefs about yourself. Or if your parent had particularly negative beliefs about love, intimacy, or relationships, you might find that you have adopted some of those beliefs too.

The final way of challenging limiting beliefs is to ask yourself objective questions concerning them. In psychology this is known as Socratic questioning, named after Socrates, who developed a method of getting to answers by asking questions. A few objective questions that you can ask concerning your limiting beliefs are

- Is there another way of looking at this?
- Does this belief match reality?
- Are you being fair to yourself?
- Are you basing this belief on new or old information?
- Is the belief based on how you feel or what you know?
- Does this belief show an unrealistic standard you might be holding onto?
- What would happen if you continued to look at life this way?
- Would someone else draw the same conclusion? Would they look at things differently?

Be mindful of the urge to defend the belief. This is common and expected during a paradigm shift. Remember, at a point in time, this belief made you feel safe or helped you make sense of life. A part of you still feels indebted to the belief, and you may feel the need to defend it.

When this urge arises, pause from the exercise and take a few deep breaths. Bring your awareness to the urge and rate its intensity. Take a few more deep breaths and rate the intensity again until you no longer feel its presence. You can then return to the exercise.

Step 5: Make a Decision

After challenging your limiting beliefs, you have a choice to make. If there was substantial factual evidence found, you can reasonably assume that the belief is accurate, which means it matches reality. Perhaps it seems limiting because it has negative undertones, but since life can be difficult sometimes, it is normal to be critical.

If you find that the negative undertones bother you, consider rephras-

75

ing the belief in a positive way. For example, instead of believing that "Not everyone has good intentions for me," which is a true statement, you can believe that "Everyone has a different colored heart." The core message is the same, but the updated version has less negative undertones.

In contrast, you may find little to no factual evidence to substantiate your limiting belief. In this case, you are safe to assume that it is inaccurate and doesn't match reality. The best way forward is to replace the belief with one that is fair and balanced.

For example, instead of believing that "I can't sustain healthy relationships," which is found to be a false statement, you can believe that "I sometimes let my anxiety get in the way of building strong relationships." The updated version can be proven true with facts, yet it still provides you with enough room to change your behavioral patterns.

After making a decision, go a step further and create an action plan on how you can respond better to similar situations that might trigger the same limiting beliefs. For instance, what exercises or actions can you take to remind you of the new and updated beliefs? Do you need to step aside and practice positive affirmations? Pull out a note from your pocket or read an encouraging quote or passage from your phone? Have the relevant tools ready and on hand because you never know when the limiting belief may be triggered.

Key Takeaways

- It isn't helpful to look at limiting beliefs as being good or bad because at some point in your life they were important for survival. Instead you might look at them as being helpful or harmful for the current life stage you find yourself in.
- Paradigm shifts don't happen every day. They usually occur when maintaining the status quo becomes too uncomfortable. We can describe a paradigm shift as questioning beliefs that were previously seen to be true and replacing them with those that align with your current worldview.
- The best way to facilitate a paradigm shift is to undergo a process known as cognitive restructuring, which is the ability to evaluate and challenge existing thought patterns. The aim of this process is to find enough evidence for or against a belief so that a positive replacement can be found and reinforced.

6

Heal Your Inner Child

*"She held herself until the sobs of the child inside subsided entirely.
I love you, she told herself. It will all be okay."*

— H. RAVEN ROSE

In this chapter you will learn:

- An introduction into inner child therapy
- Signs of a wounded inner child and the importance of inner child healing
- Steps to heal the inner child and begin the lifelong process of reparenting

Who Is the Inner Child?

In psychology, there is a concept known as inner child therapy, which describes a type of healing intervention that involves reconnecting with younger versions of yourself. The inner child is symbolic of the child version of you that exists in memories. Many believe that the age of your inner child is determined by the age when your emotional development was hindered, such as when a traumatic event occurred and you could no longer experience the world the same.

Inner child therapy allows you to have conversations with this metaphoric child, learn more about your early childhood development, and perhaps piece together the puzzle about your life. Inner child therapy can also be a great way to discover who you are, what your interests are, what you deeply care about, and what makes you so unique. Your most authentic qualities, talents, and aspirations were displayed more strongly when you were an uninhibited child, before you were conditioned to think and behave a certain way.

The idea of an inner child may sound quite childish to some people. They might perceive the concept of reconnecting to a younger self as a sign of not letting go of the past. But what is an adult if not a grown-up child? The truth of the matter is that you are a collection of "selves" that have adapted to the different stages of life and evolved to who you are today. Your inner child has played a big role in shaping the individual you are today—and he or she will continue to influence how you integrate the past with your present and future.

When you fail to establish a relationship with younger versions of yourself, you are unable to access wisdom about who you truly are and the source of the pain you are carrying. Don't be fooled into thinking just because the inner child is a much younger version of you that it is naive. Remember, that little boy or girl survived 100% of the highs and lows you experienced as a kid. Not only are they incredibly resilient, but they also have a wealth of life experience to teach you.

Author Tara Bianca, who wrote the book *The Flower of Heaven*, has a quote that says, "Children are closest to God. They reveal creation. They are the embodiment of love and connection" (Goodreads, n.d.). That childlike innocence, purity, youth, and openness that you naturally displayed as a child is what kept you going when everything around you seemed unstable.

It is unfortunate that with the passing of time, these qualities are lost or forgotten because they are what facilitate healing. The purpose of inner child therapy is to recapture those golden moments of childhood, find closure from past hurts, and commit to a lifelong journey of nurturing the inner child.

Taking a Closer Look at Inner Child Healing

Inner child healing is another interesting concept. The aim is to address unprocessed emotional wounds through communicating and responding to the unmet needs of the inner child. Once again, the assumption is that the inner child holds the answers about what exactly happened many years ago and what steps need to be taken in order to get closure and heal.

Another goal for inner child healing is to address current behavioral and relationship issues, which may be causing conflict in your life. The assumption made here is that these unwanted patterns are a result of a wounded inner child who seeks attention through projection.

For example, when you are misunderstood by a colleague, the wounded inner child might be triggered to believe that you are being disrespected, which could be a familiar emotion the child grew up experiencing. Thus, you may respond to the situation with an overly emotional response that may not be an accurate representation of what's actually happening.

A wounded inner child is like a toddler throwing a temper tantrum. It can be difficult to reason with the toddler and show them their shortcomings. The only thing the toddler cares about is expressing how they feel and getting what they want.

By giving the inner child attention and responding to its outbursts with compassion, you can begin the process of healing his or her wounds. Your inner child wants to know that somebody cares about the pain he or she has suffered and that their complex thoughts and emotions are valid. As the wounds heal, and you learn healthier ways to cope with triggers, the child won't feel the need to project negative thoughts and feelings anymore.

One of the barriers that get in the way of inner child healing is the inability to bring up past suffering from a subconscious level to a conscious level, where you can reflect upon and evaluate your thoughts and feelings. This isn't due to a lack of tools, since techniques like meditation, visualization, and journaling can help you access your subconscious mind. The issue has more to do with the internal walls you may erect that make it difficult to accept or spend time thinking about past suffering.

While it is understandable why you would build internal walls and protect yourself from confronting painful past situations, this type of coping mechanism also prevents healing from taking place. You cannot let go of something that you are still clinging onto for dear life. Healing involves facing the fears and failures of the past and the willingness to move on from that dark and lonely place.

If you believe you may have internal walls that are preventing you from fully embracing inner child healing, here are four strategies that can lower resistance and increase self-acceptance:

- **Become acquainted with your pain.**

Pain is not a curse word. It isn't something you ought to fear or distance yourself from. Every human being experiences pain, whether it is physical or psychological, due to the unpredictable nature of life.

Being ashamed of your pain causes you to disconnect with a vulnerable aspect of you that is crying out for nurturing and support. Instead of turning your back on your pain, the loving response would be to lean in.

Becoming acquainted with your pain is about displaying a commitment to understand your past and how certain events and experiences have left you with emotional wounds. The purpose isn't to blame anybody or retraumatize yourself but instead to acknowledge the tragic and painful situations that you have been through and show yourself compassion.

- **Show self-compassion.**

Self-compassion is an act of kindness directed to yourself. Most of the time, we think that kindness is an external job, something that must be shown to others. But true kindness starts from within. After all, how can we respond lovingly to others when we don't give ourselves the time of day?

Since the memories of the past can be filled with a lot of regret and shame, self-compassion is required to be able to sit with your limiting beliefs and embrace those uncomfortable emotions. You can also think of self-compassion as your defense against negative self-talk or internalized guilt.

The message that is repeated is simple: You are only human. There is only so much control you have over your world or only so much strength or courage you can display in a given situation. Like anybody else, you have good and bad days—neither of them should define who you are. Self-compassion is the reminder to continue challenging thoughts that promote perfection, self-doubt, self-sabotage, or a victim mentality.

- **Learn how to genuinely love who you are.**

If you were raised in an environment where you were not affirmed or given regular positive reinforcement, it is likely that you grew up feeling confused about who you are.

The easiest person to control is the person who doesn't have a strong connection to themselves. This not only makes you vulnerable to manipulation, but you can also become easily controlled by your own thoughts and behaviors.

One of the reasons you may have internal walls is that you don't trust yourself. The walls are there to provide an extra protective measure against outsiders because you don't trust your own judgment. The lack of self-trust is a limiting belief that controls your interactions with others. If you had a strong connection to yourself, there wouldn't be a need for this type of belief.

Self-love seeks to fill the holes that your parents could not fill as a child. The goal of self-love is to become your own source of positive reinforcement, so that you don't depend on the inconsistent validation of others.

Another component of self-love is self-awareness, which is the ability to deeply know yourself. If you have ever had a deep romantic connection with someone, you will know that real love is built over time. The more you get to know a person, the stronger your feelings become.

Self-awareness facilitates self-love by strengthening the connection you have with yourself. How can you sincerely say that you love yourself if you are detached from your personal life experiences?

- **Give yourself permission to play.**

Finally, you can lower your internal walls and increase self-acceptance by giving yourself permission to play.

It might be strange that you would need permission to play, but many adults sometimes forget that their imagination and playful nature doesn't die during puberty. It lives on inside of them, appearing as flashes of inspiration, youthful energy, innovative thinking, and the search for adventure.

Tapping into your imagination allows you to access the subconscious mind and raise your level of consciousness. You are able to embrace ideas that are contrary to the norm, which might challenge your conventional thinking.

This is necessary during the work of inner child healing because the messages your inner child may convey won't always be conventional.

For example, he or she might express the need for others to always say they are sorry when they hurt his or her feelings. The chances of this happening all of the time are slim, but your inner child may not be able to consider the practicalities.

Nevertheless, by using your imagination, you can find creative ways of fulfilling this need. Perhaps what the inner child is actually seeking is to feel respected. You can help them feel respected by setting firm personal boundaries and being unapologetic about what you need. This way, you are more likely to surround yourself with people who can take accountability for their wrong actions and apologize.

Giving yourself permission to play is also about making time for having fun. What you consider fun at your age may look different from what you consider fun at seven years old. But what matters is that you are embracing the free-spirited nature of a child that can calm your anxiety, reconnect you to your heart's desires, and allow you to live in the most authentic way.

Three Steps to Heal the Inner Child

Your inner child is activated whenever you think, feel, or sense things that remind you of your childhood. Surprisingly, this happens frequently because you are always encountering people, places, and situations that trigger memories and emotions.

You may be wondering how inner child therapy can help you heal your attachment style. By healing your inner child, you can positively change your response to anxiety triggers that arise in relationships.

Instead of reacting to your impulses—which is how the wounded inner child responds—you can seek to understand the underlying problem or unmet need that is being communicated. Plus, you are given an opportunity to validate and show compassion toward the wounded child, instead of turning your back on them.

Before we go into the three steps to heal your inner child, it is important to clarify that the inner child isn't always throwing a tantrum. Just think back to when you were a kid: Were you angry all of the time? You may have been upset when your needs were not met, which for an anxious person is occasionally.

Therefore, as you heal your inner child, remind that little girl or boy about the happy moments of childhood, when they felt most alive, creative, and connected with others. Let your goal for inner child healing be about getting back that child-like innocence and playfulness or reconnecting to lost aspects of yourself.

There are three steps to healing your inner child: connect, communicate, and nurture. Take a closer look at each step. What type of relationship dynamic does it remind you of? Can you see the similarities with a traditional parent-child relationship?

At the center of inner child healing is the process of reparenting, which can be described as providing yourself with the nurturing you didn't get as a child. Bear in mind that there is no passing blame in this process. For instance, your focus shouldn't be on reminding yourself about the shortcomings of your caregivers. Instead your attention should be on validating your needs and building inner trust by responding appropriately.

As someone with anxious attachment, reparenting yourself can also heal neediness, people-pleasing, and codependent behaviors. All of the love and attention you previously looked for in other people, you learn to source from within. You become the highest authority figure in your life that sets the standards, holds you accountable, and helps you correct mistakes.

Now that you understand the expectation of inner child healing (i.e. learning to become your own parent), it is time for us to go through each step and practice a few exercises.

Step 1: Connect

If you didn't have a close or healthy bond with your parents, you may not be familiar with the role and duties of conscious parents. Before you can connect to your inner child, you need to think about what type of parent you would like to be.

A basic definition of a parent is a man or woman who births and raises a child. However, this definition doesn't really tell us about the attitudes, beliefs, and acceptable behaviors of a parent. Thus, you will need to create your own definition of what a parent is, what their values and beliefs are, and how they relate to their child.

To make this exercise more explorative, you can study a few individuals (fictional or real) who display positive parenting qualities. Think about their lifestyles, daily interactions with their children, and communication styles. After doing some brainstorming, write down your definition:

Recognize that as you connect, communicate, and nurture your inner child, you will do so using the approach detailed earlier. This will ensure that your inner child gets to experience what unconditional love feels like. Not only will this help you during the healing journey, but it can also begin to positively change your attachment style.

So how do you connect to your inner child? The best way to connect to your inner child is to immerse yourself in childhood memories. Your childhood memories are rich with meaning, symbolism, emotions, and wisdom. Moreover, your memories get you as close as possible to the source of pain, where your triggers and destructive beliefs are rooted.

Reflection exercises can help you recall moments from your childhood. For instance, you can complete journal prompts and describe specific events, conflicts, transitions, or relationships from your past. The aim is to strictly follow the prompt and only write about one aspect. This allows you to fully focus on the details and connect to what your inner child felt at that specific moment.

Here are a few journal prompts to get you started:

1. Describe your earliest birthday party that you can remember. How old were you? Who was in attendance? How do you remember feeling throughout the day?

2. Think about a family home you frequently visit in dreams or have many memories of living in. Describe the experience growing up in that house. Who lived there? What type of family dynamic did you have? What parenting roles did your parents take? Where did you spend most of your time?

3. Recall a childhood memory where you approached your parents (you can choose anyone) for help. How old were you? What was your problem? How did you ask for help? What was the response you were given? How did you walk away feeling?

4. Recall a childhood memory where you let your parents down. How old were you? What mistake did you make? What was the impact of your mistake? How did your parents react? How did you walk away feeling about yourself?

5. Think back to your earliest memory of feeling love. Who showed you love? In your opinion, how would you describe that type of love? Is it similar or different to your current understanding of love and how so?

Reflection exercises aren't the only way of connecting to your inner child. Another way is to engage in activities you enjoyed as a child. For example, if you want to connect to your four-year-old self, you can play Legos, doodle, or get your hands dirty in the garden.

If you want to connect to your 16-year-old self, you can dress up as them, listen to your favorite music albums from that time, or meet up with high-school friends you are still in contact with. Naturally, as you immerse yourself in the experiences of the younger version of you, you will be able to connect with the thoughts and feelings that were going through your mind at the time.

Connecting with your inner child doesn't need to happen only when you want to communicate. Sometimes you may feel like distracting yourself from your current life situation and returning to happier times in your life. Or if you suffer from abandonment issues, you may simply want to check-in with your inner child and remind them that you still care.

Step 2: Communicate

The second step in the inner child healing process is to communicate. This step usually confuses people because the inner child isn't a real human being. But communicating with the inner child is simply about talking to yourself.

Sometimes your inner child will respond through gut feelings. Take a moment to reflect on what you are sensing, then write down the message. Other times your inner child may respond through synchronicities, such as seeing signs, numbers, and symbols that answer whatever question you had posed to them.

Bear in mind that your inner child may not communicate as eloquently as you do. Since they are a child, their thoughts and feelings may be scattered, spontaneous, or incomplete. Instead of showing frustration at the confusing messages you get, learn to seek clarity.

For instance, if you receive a one word answer, you can ask your inner child to explain what they mean. If they aren't good with words, perhaps they can explain with a picture or direct you to a specific place, person, or memory that might help you piece together what they are trying to communicate.

Remember to communicate with your inner child using the approach to parenting outlined in Step 1. Speak to them how you believe a parent should speak to a child and notice how they respond to you. Here are a few questions or prompts that you can ask your inner child to get the conversation started:

1. How was life growing up?

2. Who did you admire as a child? What did you love about these people?

3. What is the best memory you have of your mother?

4. What is the best memory you have of your father?

5. What do you still find difficult to accept about your living conditions as a child?

6. What do you still find difficult to accept about your relationship with your parents?

7. What were you afraid of as a child?

8. Can you remember your childhood dreams and aspirations?

9. Did you feel supported as a child?

10. Are there any secrets you are still holding onto from your childhood?

Even though communication with your inner child doesn't have to happen all of the time, it is important to first connect before communicating. Additionally, you can switch up the tone and subject of your conversations regularly. For instance, some conversations can be upbeat, and others can be serious and heartfelt.

Remember that your inner child is still a child, and they may not enjoy having emotional and long conversations all the time. If your inner child is opposed to having emotional conversations, try bribing them with playtime or some type of reward they might like!

Step 3: Nurture

The final step is to nurture your inner child. This is an ongoing process that doesn't stop after you have healed the inner child. At some point in your childhood, nurturing suddenly stopped or was withheld by your parents. This causes a lot of trauma that continues to be felt in your adult relationships.

When you commit to reparenting your inner child, you make an agreement to be consistent with your affection and nurturing. Consistency is what you yearned for as a child and therefore what your inner child needs most.

To provide consistent nurturing, you need to be aware of what your inner child needs, what their love languages are, and how they desire to be supported. There is no point in performing acts of service when your inner child craves quality time or physical touch. Thus, it is recommended to spend enough time exploring your needs and desires.

Two basic needs that children have, which inform every other need, are security and unconditional love. Your big task is to find out the specific ways in which you feel safe and loved. Remember that you are going to be the sole person responsible for responding to these needs, so avoid thinking about how other people can show up in the same ways.

Here is a list of ways to respond to your need for security:

- Set healthy boundaries.
- Be selective about who you allow into your space or home.
- Hold yourself accountable to personal goals.
- Get regular medical examinations and invest in your mental health.
- Be careful about how much you reveal about yourself online and be selective about the content you watch.
- Prioritize your career by developing a career development plan and hold yourself accountable to it.
- Save and invest money.

Here is a list of ways to respond to your need for unconditional love:

- Refrain from being judgmental about your past or current experiences.
- Spend quality time by yourself.
- Live an active and healthy lifestyle (e.g. eat a balanced diet, get sufficient sleep, adopt a spiritual practice, etc.).
- Improve your self-talk and be quick to challenge limiting beliefs.
- Listen to and validate your thoughts and feelings.
- Find hobbies and side interests that help you alleviate stress and anxiety.
- Commit to continuous learning by reading books, taking online courses, listening to educational podcasts, etc.
- Join a community of like-minded people, so you can deepen your sense of belonging.

Nurturing your inner child also involves increasing positive thoughts and feelings about yourself. You can heal your inner child by helping them become the confident and self-assured individual they have

HEAL YOUR INNER CHILD

always wanted to be.

Increasing your inner child's confidence will also teach them to be more resilient when experiencing unpleasant situations. For example, if your attachment anxiety is triggered during the early stages of a romantic relationship, being confident can make your inner child less reactive in that situation.

True confidence takes time to develop, but these daily or weekly prompts can strengthen your sense of self-worth. Each time you respond to these journal prompts, identify something new that you haven't mentioned before.

1. I am proud of myself today because...

2. Something interesting that I learned about myself today was...

3. One person who supported me today was...

4. Today, I forgive myself for...

5. One strength that I displayed today was...

6. One weakness that I noticed and embraced today was...

Key Takeaways

- The inner child is the memory of your younger self that is ingrained in your subconscious mind. It has survived all of the pleasant and unpleasant experiences of the past, but it hasn't necessarily processed and healed from them.
- A wounded inner child makes its presence felt through emotional triggers, self-sabotage, unwanted thoughts, and unhealthy patterns of behavior. The tendency for most people is to ignore the unmet needs that are being communicated in those moments.
- Inner child healing involves showing yourself the love and attention you were robbed of as a child. This is known as reparenting, and it consists of three steps: connecting, communicating, and nurturing deeper aspects of yourself.
- Reparenting is a lifelong journey that can help you source affection and validation from within and reduce the amount of anxiety you feel in relationships. Learning to respond to your own needs takes time, but with practice you can become better.

III

Reconnecting With Yourself

7

Develop a Strong Sense of Self

"It's like everyone tells a story about themselves inside their own head. Always. All the time. That story makes you what you are. We build ourselves out of that story."

— PATRICK ROTHFUSS

In this chapter you will learn:

- The importance of developing a stable sense of self and complications that can get in the way
- How to wage war against your insecurities by winning the battle over your mind
- Steps to rewrite your life story and become your own person

The Root of Insecurities

A small child starts to develop a sense of self from the age of two. This is usually when they become conscious of being a living, breathing, human being, separate from others. As they grow older, they become aware of their thoughts and emotions, and how different stimuli affect how they feel.

This development is hampered when the child isn't able to fully grow into themselves. For example, a child who is not affirmed, nurtured, or given autonomy to think and feel how they like ends up being afraid of continuing to work on finding themselves.

We have discussed in great detail the impact of ambivalent-insecure attachment on child development. However, what we haven't fully looked at is the effects it has on building a strong sense of self.

If you grew up with inconsistent parents, you were unable to fully gain their undivided attention and affection. This unfortunately created deep rooted insecurity, which impacted how you perceive yourself.

As a child, your parents made up your entire world, but you were only a part of theirs. Subsequently, their absence or emotional neglect meant that you felt alone and unwanted most of the time.

These strong feelings might have caused you to believe that something was inherently wrong with you, that perhaps if you were another child or had a different personality or temperament, you would have a stronger connection with your parents.

Whether these limiting beliefs are true or not is not the focus. The focus is on how those beliefs justified self-destructive behaviors, which ultimately made you reject and abandon yourself too. In other words, you internalized the inconsistencies of your parents, felt ashamed of who you were, and unconsciously turned against yourself.

What many people don't understand about insecurities is that they breed self-hatred. Indeed they may start out as petty criticisms, comparisons, or self-doubt, but very soon they become perceptions that inform how you see yourself.

A child that grows up with insecurities, as a result of unmet needs, becomes an adult that feels like they are not good enough, despite being competent and responsible. They are constantly haunted by the idea of being outed as a fraud (imposter syndrome) or exposed for their vulnerabilities, which will result in being rejected once again.

Another interesting behavior of children who grow up with anxious attachment is the tendency to engage in self-destructive behaviors. This occurs due to unwanted thoughts, which trigger unwanted emotions and behaviors.

An example here could be an anxious woman who is afraid of commitment because she believes that nobody would love the 'real' her. To avoid inevitable heartache, she pulls back from partners when the relationship starts to develop, shortly after the honeymoon phase ends. The outcome? She returns to her single status and misses out on the opportunity to be genuinely loved for who she is.

Other ways that anxious people self-destruct is through binge eating, binge drinking, reckless sexual encounters, shopping addictions, pursuing troubled men or women, or staying in toxic relationships. In essence, they are drawn to any kind of behaviors that might reinforce their fears of rejection and abandonment.

Bonding With Yourself

The best way to address deep rooted insecurities is to develop a genuine relationship with yourself. Doing so will allow you to see yourself for who you are, outside of the trauma and pain you experienced as a child.

This goes beyond our traditional understanding of self-awareness, which is to be aware of your thoughts and feelings. Developing a bond with yourself is about confronting the inner critic once and for all and winning the battle over your mind.

Whether or not you are aware of it, there has always been a battle over your mind. This battle is known as social conditioning, which is the programming of people to think and behave in certain ways through the use of positive and negative reinforcement.

Your family and friends, public education system, community, media, and public figures have implicitly or explicitly participated in the programming of your mind to think and behave in certain ways. Depending on your life circumstances—like the relationship with your parents, the community you grew up in, and the messages you internalized from the media—you are wired to perceive reality in a particular way.

What this means is that your perception of yourself is rigged, and this isn't by any means your fault. It is the result of social conditioning, and the many beliefs and unconscious messages you have internalized from your environment.

Thus to win the battle over your mind and develop a genuine relationship with yourself, you will need to confront your social conditioning. This will involve reflecting on the most influential forces in your childhood, assessing the types of beliefs or messages they transferred to you, and rooting out negative programming that may affect how you see yourself and the world today.

Challenge Harmful Social Conditioning

It is a disheartening realization to know that your ideas and beliefs about life aren't entirely your own. For many decades, you have been surviving off of other people's rule books or society's definitions of "normal," and you have neglected your own truth.

A basic example of this is how you model some of the behaviors you witnessed growing up. For example, if you grew up eating dinner around a table, you might continue to eat dinner around a table even now. Or if arguments at home were resolved using the silent treatment, you may continue to resolve conflict in the same manner.

Before you completely rule against social conditioning, it is important to note that not every type of social conditioning is harmful. Just imagine how difficult it would be to get through school if there weren't specific rules, structures, and codes of conduct put in place, or how unhealthy workplaces would be if there weren't any expectations enforced. Rules dictated by external parties like parents, schoolteachers, or bosses at work aren't *all* bad, but there are some that do more harm than good.

The best way to know whether society's imposed rules or expectations are harmful is to tune into how they make you feel. Remember the

OVERCOMING ANXIOUS ATTACHMENT

inner child? That subconscious memory of your younger self? He or she intuitively knows what is good for you and what isn't. Connect with them and ask the tough questions, like which childhood messages were problematic and caused a lot of internal pain. Your inner child may bring up a few commonly accepted messages based on what you were exposed to as a child. Such messages may include things like:

- Children need to be seen, not heard.
- Girls don't play with boys.
- Crying is a sign of weakness.
- Money will buy you happiness.
- People who grow up in poverty won't amount to anything.

You can also ask your inner child specific questions based on different social aspects of your life, such as:

- **Language:** What did you learn about language and communication as a child? What were you allowed or forbidden to say? What were some of the expectations around sharing thoughts and emotions?
- **People:** What did you learn about people as a child? Who were you taught to trust and distrust? How was human nature described to you? How did you look at people who were more fortunate and less fortunate than you? What were some of the expectations around personal boundaries and interaction with other people?
- **Religion:** How was religion introduced to you as a child? What was your understanding of religion? What were some of the expectations you had to follow?
- **Career:** How was the subject of work brought up as a child? What were you taught about the purpose of work? What kinds of expectations around work were imposed on you?
- **Gender:** What did you learn about your gender as a child? What

were you allowed or forbidden to do? What were the future outlooks for a boy or girl? What type of standards were you taught to uphold?

Apart from inner child work, another way to challenge harmful social conditioning is to consider the effects of maintaining the status quo. In other words, what has it cost you to live your life based on someone else's rule book? In order to connect to a deeper part of you and feel fulfilled in your relationships, your lifestyle must align with your needs, values, beliefs, and desires. You must be engaged in activities that both excite and challenge you, feel passionate about your work, and gain value from your close relationships.

In the space provided, write a personal letter to your younger self, validating the pain they must have felt not being able to express themselves and follow their heart's desires. This isn't a forgiveness letter, although if you feel you owe that young boy or girl an apology, you can give one. The purpose of this letter is to acknowledge the opportunities of self-expression that have been missed while following the status quo.

Become Your Own Person

If you intend on winning the battle over your mind, you will need to learn how to become your own person. Fortunately, you are an adult now and can choose how to live the rest of your life. You aren't obliged to live according to any individual, group, or society's manual, except your own.

As liberating as this sounds, it can also bring about a lot of anxiety. As someone who developed anxious attachment as a child, you tend to care a lot about what people think and say. For many years, other people's beliefs or judgments have helped you make sense of your own reality. This habit was born out of the need for survival and trying desperately to maintain connection with emotionally unavailable people. However, to become your own person you will need to fight this habit and work on seeking validation from within (more on changing habits later in the book).

These are some of the strategies you can practice to develop a sense of autonomy and claim the right to think and feel the way you like.

- **Expect to be misunderstood.**

Conforming to the status quo is the only way to gain mass approval. The moment you start to become your own person, it is inevitable that misunderstandings will arise. When others are confronted with ideas or thoughts that are foreign to them, their natural instinct is to reject them. Think of this as a survival response, a way to save themselves from unwanted information.

Your attachment anxiety can be triggered when you sense rejection from others, but in those moments remind yourself that people tend to judge or criticize what they don't understand. This doesn't make you a bad or undesirable person. It simply means that there is a clash between you and the other person's or group's worldview.

- **Surround yourself with "yes" people.**

To avoid constant debates or conflict around your choice of lifestyle, what you believe, or the goals you are pursuing, surround yourself with more supporters than detractors. As you are learning to become your own person, it is important to strengthen your boundaries. Distance yourself from people who tend to undermine your values, question your decisions, or make you feel guilty for standing up for yourself. Positive environments will nurture you and provide the emotional safe space you need to practice expressing needs and wants.

- **Trust your gut instinct.**

Your gut instinct is intuitive knowing that something is right or wrong. Unlike the brain, your gut instinct isn't based on facts but rather on emotional and experiential truth. How do you know what's good for you? You simply do, and undeniably so. Practicing inner child work can help you trust that inner source of wisdom and intelligence that helps you make the right choices.

- **Dare to fail.**

Most of the harmful beliefs we learned as children are based on fear. We were told to avoid certain things, stay away from certain people, or strictly live a certain way because our parents were afraid for us or projecting their own fears. To break free from the limitations of fear, be deliberate about failing at things. Take risks that you know have a 50/50 chance of working out, then embrace the outcomes. The aim of deliberating failing at things is to challenge those childhood beliefs or messages you learned about failure and to take the opportunity to positively redefine what failure means to you.

- **Stand on principles.**

Principles are the set of values and beliefs that form the foundation of who you are and what you do. They show what you deeply care about and the quality of life you desire. Standing on principles is about anchoring everything you do on specific values and beliefs. Everything you do becomes intentional, and nothing is done "for the sake of it." A great way to practice standing on principles is to ask yourself what value or belief you are honoring with each task you perform on a daily basis. For example, what values do you honor when you take your children to school, go to work, or practice meditation? If you can't anchor a task on a specific principle, reconsider its importance in your life.

Rebuild Your Self-Esteem

An important aspect of learning who you are and being comfortable in your skin is building healthy self-esteem. We can define self-esteem as the opinion you have about yourself or your overall worth. Depending on how high or low this opinion is, you can display high or low self-confidence.

When you go out into the world, you will come across different kinds of people who have different motives in getting to know you. Some people may be drawn to your personality and intend on starting genuine relationships. Others may be interested in what you have or what you do and seek to learn or take something from you (the intention isn't always manipulative).

Then there are those who have dark personalities (i.e. narcissists, psychopaths, etc.) who are drawn to you because they seek to exploit your weaknesses. When encountering these types of people, one thing they will all want to know is who you are. Some are curious because they desire to connect and build strong bonds, while others are curious because they want to know whether you have high or low self-esteem.

In general, the higher your self-esteem, the more stable your sense of self. It is much harder for people to mistreat you when your self-esteem is high because you can draw boundaries, reaffirm your values and standards, and cut ties with unsafe people, if necessary. In other words, you don't come off needy, insecure, or seeking approval from anybody.

Growing up with anxious attachment, a healthy self-esteem is perhaps something you have had to work on over the years. Due to the dynamic of the relationship with your parents, you may not have received positive reinforcement as a child, which reminded you of your sense of worth. As an adult, you can fill that void by affirming yourself and developing positive self-talk.

There are four components of self-esteem that you can work on to improve the opinion you have about yourself. These four components are discussed in detail.

Self-Confidence

Confidence is having faith in something or someone. When you display self-confidence, you show others that you believe and can depend on yourself. In order to truly feel this way, you must find reasons to believe that you carry value. For instance, you might reflect on the contributions you make in the lives of others, the progress you are making to heal from past trauma, or the aspirational goals that give your life meaning.

Here are some reflection questions you can answer to work on your self-confidence:

1. What do you do well?

2. What personal qualities help you get along with other people?

3. What positive coping skills have you picked up and significantly improved over the past few years?

4. If you had to sit down with your younger self, what is the one thing that would make them feel proud about who you are today?

5. In what ways have you positively touched other people's lives?

Identity

Identity refers to the knowledge you have about yourself. The best way to get to know who you are is to raise your level of self-awareness. In other words, it is the willingness to introspect and identify your beliefs, fears, needs, talents, and characteristics. You can also learn more about your identity by understanding the different roles you play in life and how they reveal aspects of who you are. For instance, you may be a mother, entrepreneur, and caregiver for your parent. Each role has its own foundation of beliefs, fears, needs, etc.

Here are some reflection questions you can answer to discover your identity:

1. Describe who you are in a few sentences.

2. Does your current lifestyle support who you are and what you desire?

3. What matters most to you?

4. What are your greatest fears?

5. What are you holding on to that you need to let go of?

Competence

The third component of self-esteem is feeling competent in what you do. As much as it is important to have a high opinion of yourself, it is also important to know that others are positively impacted by you. Competence is about gaining skills and knowledge so that you can make a meaningful contribution to the world. The higher your competence, the more secure you will feel in your relationships because you have tangible evidence of your value. Moreover, you will demonstrate greater resilience when confronted with challenges, since you have a toolkit of useful skills and abilities to support you.

Here are some reflection questions you can answer to work on your competence:

1. What are some personal challenges you have overcome recently?

2. What risk have you taken within the past year or two that has paid off?

3. Describe the ways you have grown within the past five years. Which areas of your life have you seen the most improvements?

4. What are your greatest physical or mental limitations right now?

5. Describe the way you resolve conflict. How might you improve your approach?

Sense of Belonging

Humans are social creatures who thrive on a sense of community. It is important for us to feel supported and validated at home, work, and within our social circles. We also have a tendency to define ourselves by the people we enjoy being around most. We see our loved ones as a mirror reflection or extension of who we are.

You don't need to have a large support network to feel a sense of belonging. The point is being able to identify a few people whom you trust and can depend on. In some cases, these people may not be friends or family; they can be medical doctors, gym instructors, church leaders, or colleagues.

Here are some reflection questions you can answer to deepen your sense of belonging:

1. In your own words, what does it mean to belong?

2. Identify values that you believe are important in a relationship.

3. What kind of support do you desire from friends and family?

4. Describe the ideal work environment that aligns with your values.

5. How do you maintain close relationships and show up for your loved ones?

Working on these four components of self-esteem can help you better understand who you are and what kind of environments and relationships positively impact your well-being. Treat the process of building your self-esteem like an ongoing exercise so you can keep track of your growth and personal transformations. For instance, on a regular basis, you can challenge yourself to perform one behavior that boosts your self-esteem. Examples include making time for a hobby you enjoy, saying one kind thing about yourself, or showing a random act of kindness to a stranger, friend, or coworker. These small behaviors will help to build self-confidence and reaffirm your identity, competence, and sense of belonging.

Rewrite Your Life Story

The reason why you need to challenge harmful social conditioning and work toward becoming your own person is so that you can reclaim your life story!

If I had to ask you right now to briefly summarize your life story, what would you say? Would you tell me about the worst years of your life? The complicated nature of your relationship with your parents? Or about the many failures you have faced? How much of your story would focus on the happy moments of your childhood? The people who actually showed up for you? Or the achievements you have won?

When you haven't yet processed the trauma, limiting beliefs, and harmful conditioning from the past, the story you tell about your life tends to be quite depressing. You may find it difficult to look beyond the pain and feel grateful for overcoming the hardships.

A negative life story affects how you see yourself in relation to other

119

people. For instance, you might see yourself as broken, unlucky, hopeless, or not good enough. Just imagine what kind of energy you bring to relationships when your life story sounds like this. If given the chance, would you feel comfortable working alongside or being friends with someone who carried this heavy energy?

Part of connecting to yourself and being unapologetic about who you are involves rethinking how you perceive your life. When your life story changes, your attitude and mindset will follow. Bear in mind, you will still face challenges. However, the difference is that your perspective on challenges will be more encouraging, allowing you to demonstrate resilience through hard times.

You may be curious about how the process of rewriting your life story works. The aim is to identify the current narrative that replays in your mind, then adjust the storyline to position yourself as the hero—the man or woman who courageously escapes the strongholds of the past and paves the road to a positive future.

There are three main elements of rewriting your life story: introspection, cognitive restructuring, and visualization. Introspection helps you recognize what stories you are telling yourself and whether or not they are serving your greater good. Cognitive restructuring helps you challenge harmful stories that may have emerged as a result of experiencing hardship.

Visualization helps you envision the positive outcomes that could come from your life story, despite how negative it may have been. For example, while you may have suffered emotional neglect as a child, the positive outcome is that you are more sensitive and compassionate toward loved ones as an adult.

Here is an example of how rewriting a story would work, using the story of a young woman named Angela.

Introspection

Angela was determined to change a few life stories that were keeping her stuck in the past. The first was a story about the relationship with her mother as a child. One day, she sat on her bed and began reflecting about why she felt resentful about the way she was raised. She wrote down a few notes in a notebook and came up with the following story:

"I was raised by a single mother who worked two jobs. She left to go to work early in the morning while I was asleep and returned home past my bedtime. I never saw much of my mother; therefore I never felt her warmth. She didn't do what normal mothers did, like give me hugs, brush my hair, or take me shopping. All she cared about was whether I had done the chores, finished my homework, and stayed away from boys. I know what it means to have a mother who provides, but I don't know what a mother's love feels like."

Cognitive Restructuring

After doing a lot of introspection and identifying the story she would like to rewrite, Angela was ready to challenge the perception she had held for so long.

She decided to ask herself a series of questions:

1. What makes you believe your mother didn't show love?
2. How do you define love?
3. How do you believe your mother would define love?

4. What were your expectations of your mother at the time?
5. What were your mother's expectations of you at the time?
6. What might have pushed your mother to have the kind of attitude that she did?

Angela thought that these questions would be easy to answer. However, what she realized while writing about that period of her life is that she had only interpreted the events from her perspective. She hadn't stopped to consider her mother's reality and the stress that was driving her to step out of her nurturing role and provide for her family. The more she empathized with her mother, the easier it was for Angela to see the bigger picture.

Visualization

Angela's final task was to visualize the positive outcomes that came as a result of going through her situation. However, before she could do that, there were a few facts about the story that she wanted to keep, despite how sad they were. These included:

- never seeing much of her mother
- never feeling her mother's warmth as a child
- not knowing what a mother's love feels like

With these facts put aside, she could close her eyes and spend time envisioning how the situation might have positively impacted her life. In other words, what advantage would being raised in that situation—with that type of parent-child dynamic—give her?

During the first session of her visualization, nothing came up. Her confidence was slightly shattered, and doubt started to creep in.

Perhaps there were no positives that could come out of her story.

She decided to take another visualization session, but this time she invited her inner child to join. Both of them sat quietly together and journeyed deep into the mind. Suddenly, Angela had a revelation.

She was currently working as a daycare teacher, looking after children in her house. Most of the children came from single parent households, and nearly all of their parents knocked off late from work.

Angela was the substitute parent that spent more than eight hours, five days a week, with these children. For the first time in her life, it made sense to her why she chose this specific career and why it felt so fulfilling to her.

In essence, by caring for children, she was healing her inner child and closing the void she felt as a child. Even though she couldn't change the fact that she never saw much of her mother or never felt her mother's warmth, she was able to nurture children who were possibly going through the same experience as she did when she was a child.

After going through these three steps, Angela adopted a new perspective about her relationship with her mother. She admits that they didn't have a traditional mother-daughter relationship, but she empathizes with the struggles her mother was facing at the time and understands how that may have distracted or detached her from the responsibility of caregiving.

Key Takeaways

- Due to anxious attachment and other developmental factors, you may have struggled to build a healthy sense of self.
- What you needed was a consistent display of affection and positive reinforcement, but unfortunately the relationship with your parents brought on deep rooted insecurities.
- Some of the ways in which insecurities from childhood manifest in adult relationships are not being comfortable with who you are and constantly feeling the need to prove your worth.
- Rewriting your life stories and learning to question how you were conditioned to think and feel are the beginning of connecting to a deeper part of you.

8

Ask for What You Need

"From what I've seen, it isn't so much the act of asking that paralyzes us—it's what lies beneath: the fear of being vulnerable, the fear of rejection, the fear of looking needy or weak. The fear of being seen as a burdensome member of the community instead of a productive one."

— AMANDA PALMER

In this chapter you will learn:

- The role of attachment in being comfortable to ask for help
- How fear-based stories can discourage you from expressing your needs
- Five steps to communicating unmet needs with confidence

Why Is It Difficult to Ask for What We Need?

It is always the case, specifically for someone with anxious attachment, to be the one giving support rather than the one who asks for it. Have you ever wondered why that is so?

To understand where the resistance comes from, let us perform a meditation together. Settle yourself in a quiet room and follow the guidelines mentioned:

- Get into a comfortable position and relax your muscles. Allow everything to hang loosely but keep your back straight.
- Close your eyes and take a few deep breaths. Complete the box breathing exercise by inhaling through your nose for five counts, holding your breath for five counts, then exhale out of your mouth for five counts. Repeat this exercise by inhaling for five counts for three more rounds.
- Take a long breath and hold. As you exhale imagine that you were being transported back to your childhood. Go as far back as your mind is willing to go, so you can access your early memories.
- Take a few moments to orient yourself in this time period. Acknowledge how old you are, where you live, and your family situation at home.
- Visualize your younger self walking up to your dominant parent. Approach your parent slowly and tune into what that little boy or girl is thinking or feeling. Are they nervous or stressed? And how come? What thoughts are going through their mind as they approach their parent?
- Once they approach the parent, visualize your younger self making eye contact. As they look into their parent's eyes, what emotions do they sense? How comfortable are they feeling at that moment?

126

ASK FOR WHAT YOU NEED

- Next, visualize your younger self asking their parent for something. Perhaps they are asking to go to the mall, bake cookies, or go on a play date with a friend. Tune into what the child is feeling at that moment, what thoughts are running through their mind.
- Take a few deep breaths and visualize your younger self walking back slowly, until they no longer see their parent, or the house, or the neighborhood.
- Open your eyes and record your experience.

The reason why the meditation ended without hearing your parent's response is because your thoughts and emotional experience is what mattered. As a child, asking for what you needed wasn't a problem. The difficulty was in anticipating your parent's reaction and deciding to place yourself in a vulnerable position where you could be rejected.

Depending on the thoughts and emotions you felt while completing the meditation, bringing yourself to ask for help as a child was stressful. Your parent may not have been the easiest person to approach, and maybe their responses were unpredictable.

Either way, you unconsciously learned that it is better to suppress your needs than give up control and risk being disappointed. This is why asking for what you need is so difficult as an adult.

Fear-Based Stories About Asking for Help

Riding on the back of the previous chapter, what stories are you telling yourself about asking for help? What makes you so resistant to express your needs and seek assistance from others?

Take a moment to think back to early beliefs or messages you internalized with regards to asking for what you need. These are some of the common fear-based stories children create about asking for help:

1. "I'm selfish for asking for what I need."

Did you ever feel uncomfortable for having needs and then guilty for expressing them to your parents? Perhaps you felt entitled, as though you were asking for a lot and putting a strain on your parent.

2. "They will think less of me if I ask for help."

If asking for help came with shame and humiliation, it is understandable why you avoided it. To prevent rejection or feeling vulnerable, you always pretended that everything was alright.

3. "I don't want to bother anyone."

Did your parents have a tendency to guilt-trip you whenever you asked for help? Even if what you were asking for was a basic need (i.e. asking for something to eat), they blew it out of proportion and made it seem like you were asking for too much. This fear-based story can lead to the first—believing that you are selfish for asking for help.

4. "Asking for help creates uncertainty."

You may have had intimidating parents who didn't put you at ease when asking for what you need. Or you may have been raised by unpredictable parents whose "yes" today is "no" tomorrow. The inability to anticipate the outcome of asking for help brought about too much anxiety, so you preferred not to ask at all.

5. "Asking for help takes too much energy."

Think back to when you were a child. Did you have to spend a lot of time brainstorming, planning, and rehearsing how you would ask for what you need? All of this preparation may have led you to believe that asking for help is draining, which felt even worse when your requests were denied.

Even though there may be some truth to these stories, they are nonetheless limiting because they prevent you from expressing your needs regardless of the outcome. Moreover, these stories serve to confirm the deep sense of rejection you may feel inside, which makes asking for help feel dangerous.

How Not to Ask for Help

With any request, there is a possibility of being turned down. That is simply the nature of asking for help. It would be unfair to expect people to say "yes" or avail themselves every time you need a helping hand.

Rejection sensitivity tends to make hearing "no" seem like the worst possible outcome. But it isn't. No is a boundary that informs you when another person has reached their personal limits. It protects them from overextending themselves and later feeling resentful about it.

Therefore, when you hear a no, avoid thinking that there must be something wrong with you. On the contrary, the boundary has nothing to do with you but everything to do with how the other person is choosing to take care of themselves.

The possibility of being turned down shouldn't stop you from communicating your needs, especially when you are committed to responding to the needs of others. You owe it to yourself to ask for the love, support, and encouragement you generously show others.

Albeit, asking for what you need is not as simple as you think. There are so many opportunities for misunderstanding when asking for help. In most cases, it isn't so much what you ask for that raises eyebrows, but how you ask for it.

People tend to remember how you made them feel, not what you said. The emotional feedback they get from you can determine how they feel about your request. A typical example is a parent yelling at their teenager for not completing house chores. Their intention is to motivate the kid to get up quickly and start on them, however the manner in which the request is communicated has the opposite effect.

Have you ever found yourself asking for what you need, then having to debate and defend why you need it? You may have been caught off guard by the aggressive response to your request because all you wanted was a simple yes or no. But what if I told you that the outcome could have been different if you communicated your needs better?

Here are some of the common mistakes that people make when asking for what they need:

1. Being overly understanding
Every relationship benefits from demonstrating empathy. It is only when you can fully step into another person's shoes that you can understand their worldview. However, when you overdo empathy, it can make it difficult to express your needs with clarity and conviction.

For example, you might need support from your partner because you are going through a hard time but hesitate to ask for it because you know how defensive they can be. You think about all of the ways in which they can misinterpret your need as a sign of not being good enough as a partner. Since you don't want to upset them, you decide that you don't really need support as much as you thought (which of course isn't true).

2. Being apologetic

Another mistake people make is to apologize profusely before, during, and after they have made a request. It might sound like this, "I'm sorry to bother you, but I really need you to send me the proposal before Friday. I'm sorry, I wish we didn't have such a short deadline."

There is a difference between apologizing for a mistake or inconvenience caused, like saying you are sorry for arriving late or asking for a favor at short notice. However, when you are respectful of other people's boundaries and are well within your rights to ask for help, there is no need to apologize.

To the person listening to your request, being overly apologetic makes you sound unsure of yourself. They are more likely to question why you need the help because you don't show any sense of conviction.

3. Using disclaimers

Many of us believe that if we make the request seem more attractive, the other person will likely agree to help us. This is why we tend to add disclaimers and other embellishments to our requests. A typical disclaimer might sound like, "I hate to have to ask you for this, but..." or "Don't get upset with me, but..."

The issue with using disclaimers is that they project a lack of confidence and, in some cases, can become self-fulfilling prophecies. For example, mentioning the idea that someone might be upset with what you are going to ask can negatively impact how they receive the news. The thought of being upset or inconvenienced has been planted in their mind, and now they have no other choice but to react with frustration.

4. Using reverse psychology

Have you ever exaggerated the size of a favor to make the other person believe that it isn't that big or difficult to perform? This is a classic example of reverse psychology, which is technically a form of manipulation.

For example, you might say, "I have such a huge favor to ask you. May you please pick up tomatoes from the grocery store on your way home?" or "This issue is going to require an expert, and I don't have the money for that right now. Do you know anyone who could quickly assist me?"

Since asking for help using reverse psychology is passive-aggressive, there is a chance that the other person may not catch on to what you are hinting at. When they do, they may get frustrated at the double message, which doesn't clearly communicate what you need.

5. Playing the victim

Another incorrect way to ask for help is to play the victim, such as sharing your personal struggles or how unfairly others have treated you. The reason why many people don't respond favorably to supposed victims is because they fail to take responsibility for their lives.

While mistakes happen and everyone faces their own fair share of suffering, it isn't right to use negative past experiences as bait to get others to respond to your needs. It is far more respectable to show a sense of independence and accountability, so others are confident that their support will make a positive difference in your life.

Five Golden Rules When Asking for Help

Now that you know what not to do, here are a few golden rules when asking for what you need. These are direct and assertive tips that you can practice whenever you make requests.

Rule 1: Commit to the request. Asking for anything requires confidence and conviction. It is important to show the other person that you are serious about having this need met, even if they end up turning you down. Showing commitment to the request conveys self-respect, and when you respect yourself, others are obliged to respect you too.

Rule 2: Understand the weight of the request. Be mindful of the gravity of what you are asking for. Consider who might be impacted, how much time and energy may be required, what skills may need to be deployed, etc. When you consider the impact, you can be more realistic and considerate of the next person.

Rule 3: Silence the inner critic. Before making a request, take a moment to silence the inner critic. Remind yourself that the outcome isn't about you. While you are in control of asking for your needs to be met, you have no control over how the other person might respond. Complete a short breathing exercise or meditation to calm your mind before approaching the individual.

Rule 4: Leave your expectations at the door. Don't attach yourself to any particular outcome. For instance, you might prefer being assisted with Option A, but the individual might only be able to assist you with Option B. What matters is that you are receiving help, meaning that your needs are being met—regardless of how it may look. A great way to manage your expectations is to regularly meditate on what you are grateful for. Allow the spirit of gratitude to be evident in the way you live and approach life.

Rule 5: Believe in yourself. Do you believe that you deserve to be helped? This question is of utmost importance because it shows whether or not you are open to receiving help. If you don't believe you are worthy of having your needs met, you may not be as confident and assertive in making requests, which unconsciously sabotages your opportunity to receive help. Spend time working on improving your sense of self-worth, so you are able to stand up for what you need.

BLOOM

There are times when asking for what you need is easy and other times when it feels uncomfortable. For instance, you may not have any trouble asking a friend to drive you to the airport, lend you money, or look after your pet for a few days. But whenever your needs involve communicating boundaries, the same cannot be said.

It is understandable why you get hesitant to set limits with loved ones or express unmet needs. The process of communicating your needs reveals your inner thoughts and feelings, which makes you feel vulnerable. You would like to assume that your close friends and family know how to respond to your needs without you having to remind them or that what you need is common sense, thus when others cross your boundaries, they are doing so deliberately. Unfortunately, these assumptions aren't true.

Communicating your need for space should be as easy as communicating your need for an apology or respect. This is because all of these needs are connected to your core values. When your loved ones honor your needs, they are essentially honoring you, and the opposite can be said when your needs aren't met. Therefore, as a sign of self-respect, you have every right to express unmet needs, including those that you would classify as embarrassing. Despite how awkward it may feel defending your needs, it proves how much you value them.

With that being said, there are five steps that you can follow when communicating unmet needs. These steps are summarized in the acronym BLOOM, which stands for

- Branch
- Label
- Open
- Own
- Make

What follows is an outline of the steps and how you can practice them.

B: Extend an Olive Branch

Whenever you are approaching someone for a serious conversation, such as expressing unmet needs, there is always a possibility of conflict arising.

To put the other person at ease, you can start the conversation by extending an olive branch. This can be a simple sentence or two that allows them to feel seen. For example, you might say, "Thank you for making time to listen to what I have to say."

On the lines, practice different ways of extending an olive branch.

Write a few sentences that you can use in real life situations.

L: Label the Feeling

It isn't common to start a conversation by putting your emotions on the table. However, emotions tend to be what gets in the way of addressing the real issues. It is best to lay down your feelings from the get-go and allow the person time to process your emotional experience throughout the discussion.

Since the emotions are what you feel inside as a result of your unmet needs, use "I feel" or "I felt" statements to show ownership and avoid projection or passing blame. An example of an "I" statement would be "I have been feeling embarrassed whenever you put me on the spot in front of our friends."

Think of a few scenarios in the past where you were offended by friends or family. Based on those scenarios, create some "I feel" statements.

O: Open Up

Most people stop at expressing how they feel, but that doesn't provide enough context to allow the other person to empathize. It is important to really think about the impact of having an unmet need, beyond the temporary emotion that is triggered.

You can choose how much information you are comfortable sharing with the person about your personal needs. For example, if you are addressing a friend you don't know very well, you might say "I know you don't have bad intentions, but I have experienced bullying in social circles before, and it typically followed the same pattern."

If it is a friend you trust and feel comfortable opening up to, you might show more vulnerability by saying "I know you don't have bad intentions, but whenever you do that it triggers anxiety from being bullied by ex-friends." It is important to use your discernment when deciding how much to share so that you don't feel overly exposed.

Using the examples from the previous steps, choose a few experiences to open up about. Imagine that you are speaking to someone you don't know very well and someone whom you trust.

O: Own Your Ask

The fourth step is to make a request. Fortunately, you have already learned a lot about making requests, but a great tip to remember is to show conviction. You can show conviction by being clear and direct about your ask.

Mention step-by-step what you would like the person to do in order to fulfill your needs. Ideally, they should leave without feeling confused about what you want. Here is an example: "Moving forward, I would like for you to not make jokes at my expense, even if you think they are harmless."

Remember that conviction isn't the same as rudeness or arrogance. You can be firm and direct, while being considerate of the other person's feelings. Avoid making threats, snide remarks, or impolite statements that might cause the person to stop listening or caring about what you have to say.

On the lines, practice making requests with conviction. Look at each request and ask yourself if you would be comfortable being told the same thing.

M: Make It Specific

The final step gives you an opportunity to clarify what you need. In other words, making real life examples so that the person knows what you specifically want. When making examples, ensure that they are relevant to your relationship dynamic. Use situations that occur on a daily basis. Here is an example: "When I say, 'making jokes at my expense,' I mean using my personal stories or comments that I have made as something to mock in front of other people."

Using the responses from the previous step, take the opportunity to provide more clarity by offering examples:

If we had to put these five steps together, we would have the following:

"Thank you for making time to listen to what I have to say. I have been feeling embarrassed whenever you put me on the spot in front of our friends. I know you don't have bad intentions, but I have experienced bullying in social circles before, and it typically followed the same pattern.

Moving forward, I would like for you to not make jokes at my expense, even if you think they are harmless. When I say, 'making jokes at my expense,' I mean using my personal stories or comments that I have made as something to mock in front of other people."

Can you sense how clear, confident, and committed that request was? This is the goal that you will work toward as you learn to be more vocal about unmet needs.

Key Takeaways

- Every human being has needs, but some hide them better than others. Your openness or resistance toward asking for what you need has a lot to do with how responsive your parents were as a child.
- Take a moment to reflect on where the resistance is coming from. Think deeply about the fear-based stories you may be telling yourself about expressing your needs.
- Remember that there is a right and wrong way to ask for help. Some of the wrong ways include being overly empathetic, using disclaimers, or practicing reverse psychology. The right ways involve committing to your ask, leaving your expectations at the door, and believing in yourself.

- Communicating unmet needs can be difficult, but you owe it to yourself to stand up for the things that matter to you. The BLOOM five-step framework can teach you how to clearly and assertively express unmet needs and what you desire moving forward.

9

Which Direction Are Your Habits Taking You?

"We change our behavior when the pain of staying the same becomes greater than the pain of changing. Consequences give us the pain that motivates us to change."

— DR. HENRY CLOUD & DR. JOHN TOWNSEND

In this chapter you will learn:

- How childhood attachment patterns continue into adulthood, and how to confront them
- The science behind habit formation, as well as discovering why unhealthy behaviors bring rewards to the brain
- How to use the NLP pain and pleasure principle to break unhealthy behavioral patterns

You Are What You Repeatedly Do

Tabitha was raised by strict, emotionally unavailable parents who had high expectations for her to live up to. She was often ridiculed for crying, expressing fears, or asking for help. This caused her to mature very quickly and develop a thick exterior.

As she grew older, Tabitha developed an unconscious preference for men who were emotionally unavailable. She interpreted this as being introverted and mysterious, but this was far from the truth.

Her boyfriends were incapable of holding emotional space for her. Whenever she would express how she felt, they would somehow change the topic or trivialize what she was going through. Tanya would get upset, close herself in the room, and come out when she was feeling better. Eventually, she married one of these men and experienced the same cycle of emotional invalidation in her marriage.

Pete, on the other hand, was raised by overprotective parents. He was an only child, and his parents treated him like a young prince. The only issue was that Pete was never allowed to make decisions for himself. His controlling parents did most of the thinking and feeling for him until it was time to go to college.

At college, Pete discovered he had an unconscious preference for women who were domineering. These were the type of ladies who wanted to be involved in every aspect of his life. Occasionally, Pete would get frustrated and attempt to stand up for himself. However, his message would often come out unclear because he hadn't practiced sharing his thoughts and feelings as a child.

143

Pete grew to have a negative view of women and relationships in general. He saw women as controllers who didn't have his best interests at heart. But this didn't stop him from being attracted to women that reinforced the same patterns he saw growing up.

Have you ever found yourself feeling frustrated because you kept repeating the same unhealthy behaviors and getting the same results? Like Tabitha and Pete, you may have a "type" that is reminiscent of the attachment with your parents.

Repeating the same patterns over and over again is not a conscious process that you can control. The cues happen on a subconscious level, which means that you often wake up during or after the pattern or cycle has taken place. The best way to break unhealthy patterns is to understand how they were formed in the first place, then reprogram your mind to accept healthier patterns.

The Science Behind Your Habits

How many times have you looked in the mirror and said the words "This is the last time?" At the moment, you sincerely believed that you were bidding farewell to toxic behaviors and venturing on a new and healthier path. After a week or month, you somehow found yourself performing the same behaviors.

Was the mirror speech just an act? Or could you have overlooked a crucial component of behavioral change-habit formation? We can define a habit as a behavior carried out consistently over time. The part of your brain that is responsible for habit formation is known as the basal ganglia, which also assists with other brain functions like emotion processing and pattern recognition.

The reason for having a separate region of the brain that assists with forming habits is that without learned behaviors, the brain would be too overwhelmed with processing new information each day. Just imagine if you had to learn how to brush your teeth, hold a knife and fork, or drive your car every day, as though you hadn't done it before. How different would your life have been?

As much as you need habits to progress in life, there are some that don't serve you. These tend to be unhealthy habits that reinforce unwanted thoughts, emotions, and behaviors. Habits related to past trauma, emotional triggers, limiting beliefs, or low self-esteem can be classified as unhealthy and unproductive.

The type of habits you need to live a fulfilling life and build meaningful relationships should be helpful and encouraging. But breaking unhealthy habits isn't as simple as looking into a mirror and announcing that you quit. In order to break unhealthy habits, you need to make changes to the brain.

Fortunately, the brain is capable of learning and unlearning behaviors through a process called neuroplasticity. This process typically happens naturally as you are exposed to new experiences, however you can activate the process through what is called self-directed neuroplasticity (retraining your brain to create and enforce new patterns).

The Pursuit of Pleasure

The science behind how the brain forms habits is quite interesting. The main idea is that the brain is wired to seek pleasure and avoid pain. This very simple programming is what has kept our human species alive. Actions that bring pleasure are seen as safe and beneficial, while those that bring pain are seen as threatening and undesirable.

You can test this biological instinct in your own life by reflecting on the tasks you most enjoy and those you put off or conveniently forget about. You can also consider how long it takes for you to learn and memorize tasks that you enjoy compared to tasks that you dislike.

The brain has a sneaky way of persuading you to spend time doing pleasurable activities. Whenever you complete a task that you enjoy, you are rewarded with a good feeling. The good feeling is a release of the brain chemical dopamine, which has the same sedative effects as morphine. The release of dopamine motivates repeating the same pleasurable behaviors, over and over again, until eventually they become habits.

Nevertheless, there is a catch. As evolved and sophisticated as the brain is, it cannot differentiate between healthy and unhealthy behaviors; it can only tell the difference between behaviors that bring pleasure and those that bring pain. Essentially, this means that unhealthy behaviors which bring pleasure can become habits.

You might be wondering to yourself how something bad for you can make you feel good. For some reason, that idea sounds contradictory. Let us return to the examples of Tabitha and Pete to answer this question. If you recall, both Tabitha and Pete had attachment issues that trace back to childhood. Tabitha had emotionally unavailable parents, and Pete had overprotective parents.

Neither Tabitha nor Pete felt secure in the relationships with their parents. In fact, they spent the majority of their childhoods suppressing needs and finding different ways to cope with the inconsistent parenting. But shockingly, in their adult relationships, they played out the same attachment patterns!

Why on earth would Tabitha and Pete feel attraction toward partners who reinforced the same unhealthy relationship dynamics they experienced as children? Wouldn't they want something better for themselves? The truth is that despite how unhealthy their childhood attachments were, they felt familiar. For 18 years or so, their brains were trained to accept hot and cold behaviors. They learned to accept that unrequited love is normal, and a mutual give-and-take is abnormal.

Therefore what felt "safe" were partners who would love them the same way they were loved as children, and what felt "threatening" were partners who would challenge their understanding of love—even if challenging the pattern was for their own good.

As someone who grew up with anxious attachment, what you perceived as normal interactions and bonding may not be what is healthy for you. However, the patterns have already been formed in your brain, and until you change them, you are wired to continue practicing habits that feel "safe" even if they are destructive.

It would be easy to just look in a mirror and declare the patterns gone. But that isn't enough to break a habit and create new patterns. You will need to go through the process of self-directed neuroplasticity and retrain your brain to distinguish between behaviors that bring pain and those that bring pleasure.

Rethinking Pain and Pleasure With NLP

Neuro-linguistic programming (NLP) is a type of therapy that seeks to retrain your mind on how to think. It consists of three components:

- **Neurology:** Understanding and recognizing the mental processes and patterns of the subconscious mind.
- **Linguistic:** Using language to make positive suggestions to the subconscious mind.
- **Programming:** Approaching the mind like an internal operating system that can be updated whenever it receives new inputs.

As mentioned earlier, the best way to break unhealthy habits is to update the patterns that inform your behavior. This can be done through self-directed neuroplasticity using therapies like NLP.

Currently, your internal operating system (brain) is programmed using a specific "language." It can only understand messages that are processed in this specific language. Whenever you try to introduce messages using a foreign language, it simply rejects the suggestion. Therefore, before you can switch languages, you must spend time teaching your brain how to recognize the new language.

Perhaps your current language reinforces unhealthy behaviors that aren't bringing the results you desire in life. While reading this book, you have discovered a better language that you would like to teach your brain, which promotes healthier behaviors. NLP can help you make suggestions to your subconscious mind that can effect changes on a neurological level.

One of the most powerful ways to make suggestions to the subconscious mind is to use an NLP technique known as the pain and pleasure principle, or leverage. The aim of the principle is to motivate positive behavioral change by using both pain and pleasure.

In the previous section, we discussed the brain's natural response to pain and pleasure. It has been biologically programmed to avoid pain and seek pleasure as a way of survival. However, NLP teaches that both pain and pleasure can be beneficial to improving overall well-being.

For example, the pain of surviving a difficult childhood can create a desire for a peaceful and healthy lifestyle, or the pain of loneliness can motivate you to seek companionship. The motivating factor behind pleasure is obvious. You are drawn to aspirational goals because they promise an idealistic life.

Central to the pain and pleasure principle are emotions. Your emotions about certain situations are what drive you to seek change. Unpleasant emotions are just as effective as pleasant emotions because they create a strong desire. For example, being afraid that you can't trust anyone can generate enough motivation to work through your trust issues. In other words, even negative sensations or experiences can be used as leverage to change the way you think and approach life.

The trick, however, is to increase the intensity of your emotions to the extent that they create urgency, such as the need to take action NOW. Going back to the example of trust issues, unless you feel really grieved that you are unable to trust people, you might not be motivated to take the steps to heal. Connecting to the "why" behind your emotions can also help to increase the intensity and make the problem feel very real and serious.

Think back to the times in your life when you were driven to take action because of the fear of losing someone, being evicted from your home, suffering financially, or jeopardizing relationships that were most important to you. Even though that fear was extremely uncomfortable, you were able to make swift decisions and step outside of your comfort zone. This enables you to break out of habits and engage in new behaviors.

The benefit of using the pain and pleasure principle when breaking unhealthy habits is that it doesn't require you to have discipline. All it requires is for you to want something so badly that you are driven to disrupt existing behavioral patterns.

While discipline is an excellent skill to learn, it requires a lot of conscious effort. For instance, the way to increase discipline is to do those things that you dislike, over and over again, regardless of how you feel. When using this approach, your brain (which is constantly looking for a dopamine hit) will resist many times, making the process uninspiring.

The pain and pleasure principle works in a subconscious way and doesn't require you to think about doing those things that you dislike or that seem hard. Your only focus is to spend time intensifying your emotions (positive or negative) so that you feel a passion or strong pull to commit to change.

There are three steps you can practice to work on breaking unhealthy patterns using the pain and pleasure principle.

Step 1: Objectively Observe Your Current Behavioral Pattern

Before you begin making suggestions to the subconscious mind, take the time to assess the behavioral pattern you would like to change. This can be done through meditation or journaling. The aim is to reflect on the habit, when it is triggered, how it manifests, etc. Do your best to be as neutral and objective as possible, so that you can see the full picture without being clouded by emotions.

You are welcome to use the lines for journaling.

_____

_____

_____

_____

_____

_____

_____

_____

_____

Step 2: Tune in to Your Feelings

Now that you are familiar with what is happening, it is time to charge your mind with emotions. You can choose whether to focus on the pain or pleasure associated with the habit.

For example, you might focus on the pain of losing something/someone or ending up in a worse state if you continue reinforcing the pattern. Or you can focus on the pleasure of being physically, mentally, and emotionally freed from the pattern.

It can also help to ask yourself deep questions associated with the pain or pleasure. Here are a few questions that can help you intensify the pain:

- What are the consequences of repeating this pattern for another 5–10 years?
- What will you lose if you don't change?
- What opportunities will you miss out on if you don't change?
- How much worse has the pattern gotten over the years?
- Here are a few more questions that can help you intensify the pleasure:
- How would you feel if you successfully overcame the habit?
- What opportunities would you qualify for after breaking the habit?
- How different would you feel about yourself and your relationships?
- What would your life look like in 5–10 years if you chose to break the habit right now?

Spend several days or weeks on this step. Repetition is key when it comes to making changes on a subconscious level. It won't take one round or one day to change deeply ingrained patterns, but rather several attempts.

Step 3: Interrupt Current Unhealthy Pattern

While you are diligently working on intensifying your emotions, try to catch yourself whenever you are triggered to reinforce the current unhealthy pattern. The earlier you identify the trigger or behavior, the easier it will be for you to interrupt the pattern.

Interrupting the pattern is about finding a positive distraction to shift your focus on something else. For example, when you are triggered to withdraw from your partner during an argument, you can interrupt the pattern by singing lyrics to a song, smiling while looking at your partner, or anything that might reduce the urge to carry out the existing pattern.

Continue to distract yourself until you notice the urge has gone. Thereafter, proceed by carrying out your desired behavior, which might be expressing how you feel in a calm and respectful way. Reward yourself after successfully completing the desired behavior as a way of hinting to your brain that the new behavior is pleasurable and worth learning.

Another positive distraction that can help you build a secure attachment style is practicing self-care. We can define self-care as behaviors that seek to enhance your well-being and overall quality of life. These might include things like scheduling daily check-ups with yourself, working out, staying connected with close friends and family, and practicing gratitude. You can interrupt an unhealthy pattern by turning to the simplest form of self-care you can perform at that moment. Reward yourself for completing a desired behavior.

The pain and pleasure principle is not a magical tool. You will need to put in the effort to engage your mind and make strong suggestions. Once again, repetition is the only way that your brain can learn new patterns and habits.

Key Takeaways

- Unhealthy habits can make you feel powerless and compromise the quality of your relationships. But when you begin to understand that your brain's job is to recognize and reinforce patterns, you can feel more empowered to change how you think.
- Habit formation is an essential function of the brain that is controlled by the basal ganglia. Behaviors that are associated with pleasure are rewarded with a release of dopamine, which motivates repetition.
- Unfortunately, the brain cannot tell the difference between healthy and unhealthy behaviors; it only knows what feels painful or pleasurable.
- NLP's pain and pleasure principle can help you unlearn harmful patterns and program your brain to recognize healthier patterns. This is done by increasing motivation and urgency and intensifying both painful and pleasurable emotions.

10

Strive Toward Secure Attachment

"In essence, if we want to direct our lives, we must take control of our consistent actions. It's not what we do once in a while that shapes our lives, but what we do consistently."

— TONY ROBBINS

In this chapter you will learn:

- What a secure attachment feels like, and why love is the central component
- How to find people with the right companions who make you feel emotionally safe
- How to shift from codependency to interdependency and cultivate positive relationships

155

What Does Secure Attachment Feel Like?

The goal for overcoming anxious attachment is to adopt a secure attachment with loved ones. This goal is ambitious, but it is possible with the right interventions, like the ones shared in this book.

While working toward healing your attachment style, it is worth familiarizing yourself with what secure attachment feels like. After all, if you are unable to picture yourself being securely attached, you may experience trouble staying motivated to change toxic behavioral habits.

Before we go into an explanation of what to expect when you are securely attached, let us begin by completing a meditation to tune into the frequency of unconditional love. Follow these instructions (you can record the meditation yourself and listen to it if you like):

1. In a quiet area, find a comfortable place to sit and allow your body to hang loosely. Keep your spine lengthened and take deep and slow breaths.
2. When you are feeling calm, close your eyes and mentally picture your inner child (represented in a child's body) walking toward someone, real or fictional, who embodies love. This could be your grandmother, favorite pet, or a spiritual entity.
3. As your inner child gets closer, tune into what they are thinking and feeling. Don't rush the walk toward this loving figure. Take your time and connect with your inner child's excitement, nervousness, or whatever they might be going through.
4. Picture your inner child finally reaching the loving figure. What is the first thing that little boy or girl says? How do they behave around this figure? How do they express themselves?

5. Shift your attention onto the loving figure. Notice how they respond to your inner child. Do they smile, laugh, or play along? How do they make your inner child feel about him or herself? Play out the sweet interaction between the two in your mind.
6. Picture the two of them looking at each other, preparing to go separate ways. How do each of them feel at this moment? What do they desire or wish to express to one another?
7. Watch as your inner child walks back slowly from where they came from. As they walk away, what are they thinking or feeling?
8. Take a few deep breaths, and when you are ready, open your eyes and journal about the experience.

There are some who mistakenly assume that people who fall under the three insecure attachment styles are incapable of feeling genuine love. This assumption is often justified by the fact that these individuals had a rough childhood.

What they overlook is that the emotion of love is not necessarily tied to parents. Of course, in many cases, parents are the ones who expose a child to love, but they are not the gatekeepers of love. In the absence of parental love, it is possible for a child to develop loving relationships with other real or fictional entities or as an adult to grow to love themselves.

The fear of not being capable of loving others should not hold you back from opening yourself up to the possibility of love. All you need to do is look around you, and you will find people or things to love. If you are unable to develop a loving bond with another person, look to animals or nature, find hobbies and passion projects, or connect to your Higher Power.

The reason why we are speaking at length about love is because it is what enables a secure attachment. In order for two people to be securely attached, they must be open and willing to love each other. This love will look different in a platonic, romantic, or work relationship, but the intention remains the same.

The best way to describe securely attached friends, family members, or couples is: two imperfect people who are comfortable in their own skins and create a space where each of them can express who they are without judgment. An emphasis must be made on "imperfect" because there is bound to be conflict within those loving relationships. But the presence of conflict doesn't compromise the safety they have built and continue to maintain.

Now to answer the question of what a secure attachment feels like. Quite simply, it can feel like the following experiences:

- feeling a boost of energy whenever you are in the presence of other person
- being more open to trying new experiences and stepping outside of your comfort zone
- feeling comfortable sharing ideas and opinions without second-guessing yourself
- letting go of the need to control outcomes; trusting in the integrity of the relationship
- being generous with your resources, but knowing when you have reached your limits (also, not being afraid to set limits)
- maintaining your individuality and celebrating the other person's uniqueness
- feeling an inner motivation to become the best version of yourself to develop the skills necessary to maintain your relationship
- being realistic about the shortcomings of the other person; recognizing when your shortcomings are causing pain in the relationship
- accepting the fact that your relationship doesn't need to be perfect, neither do you hold each other to that standard
- living for the present moment and fully embracing the state of your relationship right now
- being committed to change, if and when your behaviors threaten the sense of safety you have both established

Find Your Tribe

As someone with anxious attachment, you may identify as having a tendency to people-please, or at least this was something you dealt with in the past. This habit stems from childhood, and it was often used as a strategy to get the attention of your parents.

Unfortunately, it has also gotten you into some sticky situations with friends and family, where you felt uncomfortable saying no or afraid to express your true personality. You may have also noticed that being a people-pleaser made you vulnerable to being used and abused.

As you work toward a secure attachment style, you will need to overcome the tendency to people-please once and for all. Since secure attachment is based on the willingness to love and be loved, you don't need to go out of your way to seek approval from others.

People who are willing to genuinely connect and develop a bond with you won't demand that you act in a certain way to get their attention. They encourage you to express who you are unapologetically and set boundaries when you have reached your limits.

Finding the right people and making the right associations can put your attachment anxiety at ease and allow you to open up without shame. However, knowing who is right for you takes a lot of self-awareness because you need to look beyond who excites you in the moment and find people who make you feel safe.

For example, as someone with an anxious attachment, you would feel safe in a friendship or romantic relationship with someone who has a secure attachment style. In some cases, relationships with another anxious person can work, however both of you would need to be self-aware and willing to talk through the uncomfortable moments when you feel triggered.

Being friends with or dating someone with an avoidant or disorganized attachment style is a recipe for disaster. Since you need a lot of reassurance in a relationship, it is important to surround yourself with people who are emotionally available and are able to create a safe space for you to express your thoughts and feelings.

People with avoidant and disorganized attachment are uncomfortable with their own emotions, let alone those of others. They may unintentionally hurt you by dismissing your feelings or shutting down when they are upset.

Characteristics of Emotionally Safe People

The right kind of people for you don't have a particular face or body. They don't have to be the same race, age, gender, or socio-economic class as you either. But one thing is for certain: They must be emotionally safe.

Throughout the book we have discussed the importance of emotional safety in the parent-child relationship. The absence of emotional safety as a child meant that you found relationships difficult to manage as an adult. Now that you are ready to build secure relationships founded on love, it is important to train your brain to be attracted to emotionally safe friends, partners, coworkers, etc.

What makes someone emotionally safe is their ability to accept others for who they are. They don't wish for you to think or feel any particular way. Moreover, they don't expect perfection or for you to always be on your best behavior. Emotionally safe people allow you to be human, and that is what makes them suitable for you.

If you are interested to know what kinds of character traits to look out for that scream "emotionally safe," there are some to consider:

- **An emotionally safe person validates your feelings.**

A sign that you are in the company of an emotionally safe person is that you feel comfortable sharing details about your life and hard emotions that you are working through and becoming emotional in front of them. They respond by listening and allowing you to process your emotions.

- **An emotionally safe person admits to being wrong.**

To qualify as being "emotionally safe," you must be self-aware, which is being able to recognize your strengths and weaknesses. When you are in a relationship with someone who is self-aware and accepts their flaws, they are able to reflect on their actions, apologize for their mistakes, and make the necessary changes.

- **An emotionally safe person is willing to grow and learn.**

Still on the subject of self-awareness, an emotionally safe person knows that there are certain aspects of their character that need improvement. This is something they are able to admit and actively work on. They are also self-motivated to change because they understand the benefits of becoming a better version of themselves (not only to strengthen your relationship, but other relationships in their life too).

- **An emotionally safe person values trust.**

Trust is an important aspect of any healthy relationship. It is the agreement two people make with each other to always act in each other's best interest. An emotionally safe person honors the trust that you have for each other. They behave in ways that allow you to feel safe in their company and when you are apart.

- **An emotionally safe person takes full responsibility for their physical, mental, and emotional well-being.**

A sign that someone is emotionally safe is taking good care of themselves. They know themselves well enough to respond to their own basic needs. Additionally, they are proactive about addressing stress and other challenges life might throw.

For instance, to manage work stress more effectively, they might start going to the gym or improving their sleep routine. This doesn't mean that they don't need you, however they never make you feel like you are responsible for their well-being.

Work Toward Interdependence

One of the benefits of cultivating emotionally safe relationships is that you can lean on the other person without feeling dependent on them. This can be a breath of fresh air after many years spent feeling like you need people in order to be happy.

A word you might hear being used when referring to healthy relationships is interdependence. Interdependence is the ability to form an emotional bond with someone, while maintaining a strong sense of self. In other words, you are invested in building the relationship but don't allow the dynamic to consume your life.

People with secure attachment tend to display interdependence in their relationships. They are able to be vulnerable without becoming needy, and they respond to the other person's needs without overextending themselves.

The opposite is true for people with anxious attachment. Since close relationships brought about a lot of anxiety, they learned to cling on to people, outsource most of their needs, and become dependent on relationships for building identity or feeling a sense of purpose.

For some people it led to developing codependency, a type of relationship where an individual's thoughts and feelings become centered around the needs and behaviors of another person. Instead of wanting to connect and maintain a strong bond, a codependent person feels the need to keep the relationship intact, even when the dynamic starts to become toxic.

Part of working toward interdependence is learning the early signs of codependency in relationships, so you can take a step back and assess your boundaries. Some of the signs to look out for include:

- You get a boost of energy when others praise you and tend to feel down when your efforts aren't recognized.
- Your moods and behaviors change depending on how your close friend, partner, or family member feels at that moment.
- You neglect your own needs and plans to show up for loved ones and make sure that they are satisfied.
- You feel anxious making decisions without the other person's advice or consent.
- You adjust your thoughts and opinions based on the perspective your loved one or colleague takes.

It is possible to change a relationship dynamic from being codependent to interdependent. However, it will require commitment from both parties. If one party refuses to change harmful behavioral patterns, the dynamic cannot be interdependent. Remember, interdependence requires self-awareness and respecting boundaries, which must be reinforced by both people.

Nevertheless, this shouldn't stop you from working on yourself and overcoming codependent behaviors. While waiting for your loved one to get on the same page, you can start developing qualities of interdependence. What follows are a few practical ways to begin the shift toward interdependence.

1. Acknowledge your part.

The first step is to acknowledge some of the behavioral patterns you have reinforced in the past that have contributed to a codependent relationship.

Write down as many behaviors as you can recall and the impact they have on your relationship dynamic.

2. Get to know yourself.

For the next few weeks and months, prioritize getting to know yourself again. Each week, set up an activity that involves introspection or doing an activity that makes you happy. The aim is to rediscover who you are outside of the relationship, so you can begin to source strength from within.

Use the lines to plan out the activities and exercises that you will complete for the next week or month.

_____

_____

_____

_____

_____

3. Practice making your own choices.

It is important to learn and be comfortable relying on yourself so that when others aren't available or willing to respond to your needs, you don't feel lost or abandoned. One of the ways to build self-reliance is to practice making decisions without seeking feedback from others. Trust in the fact that you intuitively know what is good for you; that you are capable of taking care of yourself.

Reflect on the people whom you lean on for support in decision-making. Write down a list of decisions you find difficult to make without them.

For the next week, strive toward making these decisions alone. You are welcome to seek information from the internet or blogs but refrain from relying on people you know.

4. Invest in your social life.

The benefit of having a rich and vibrant social life is that you don't have to rely on a single relationship to meet all of your needs. For example, you might set up dates with friends whenever you feel like having emotional conversations, which can relieve a lot of pressure from your romantic relationship.

Take stock of your social life and write down what you believe is missing. Do you perhaps need more like-minded friends to do social activities with? Do you need to expand your definition of "social" and try out new activities? Or do you need to make your social life more of a priority?

5. Create positive communication rules.

Part of building interdependence is creating a relationship where two people can be themselves and express their own thoughts and feelings openly. In order for this to occur, there needs to be rules put in place to guide communication.

For example, in order to feel safe expressing your thoughts and feelings, you might need the other person to

- listen without interrupting
- validate your emotional experience
- reserve their opinion until you ask
- make time for check-ins and spending quality time together

They might also have rules of their own, which you would combine with your list. It is easier to hold yourself accountable for positive communication when there are clear expectations on how to engage with each other.

Accentuate the Positive

It is not a bad thing to seek happiness from a relationship. In fact, healthy relationships support your mental and emotional well-being and enhance positive emotions.

While conflict and challenges are unavoidable, they shouldn't be the center of your relationships. Remember that relationships that feel stressful trigger your body to shut down and find alternative ways to cope. When you shut down, emotional safety is compromised, and you cannot fully be open and present in the relationship.

As a child, you didn't have a choice of how your relationships turned out. You depended on your caregivers to provide the best care they knew how. But now that you are grown and can choose who to invite into your life and the type of relationships to invest in, it is worthwhile to choose people and relationships that accentuate the positive.

Since your well-being hinges on the connections you make, seeking out positive relationships should be a priority. One of the ways to know that you are in positive relationships is to assess how you feel in the presence of the other person, and whether you become more or less of yourself. Positive relationships are not meant to change who you are, but instead they create enough room for you to feel more deeply connected to yourself.

Here is a short assessment you can do by yourself, whenever you seek to reflect on the impact that your platonic, romantic, or professional relationships have on you. For each question, respond with curiosity about how you can accentuate the positives and develop a stronger relationship.

1. Do they bring out the best in you?

A positive person tends to have an optimistic attitude toward life and relationships. As a result, they can be encouraging and complimentary. This doesn't mean that they are unaware of your flaws, but they choose to focus and comment on your strengths and positive qualities.

Reflect on whether the other person brings out the best in you. Provide evidence to support.

‑‑‑

‑‑‑

‑‑‑

‑‑‑

‑‑‑

‑‑‑

2. Can they fight well?

It is important to accept that people have a good and dark side. Yes, even the most compassionate people have character flaws. It is unfair to expect a friend, partner, or coworker to be positive all the time. However, the manner in which they respond to conflict matters.

Conflict is supposed to be an opportunity for learning who the other person is and what they want. It is a chance for both parties to express difficult feelings, seek clarity, and step into the other person's shoes.

The best way to tell if the other person fights well or not is to assess how you feel after an argument. For instance, do you avoid each other or are you able to change the topic and speak on something else?

Reflect on your arguments with the other person. Identify areas where you can both improve, such as how the fight ends or giving each other an opportunity to be validated.

3. Are you able to maintain your individuality?

A positive relationship is first and foremost a safe space to be yourself. One of the signs that you are in a positive relationship is being free to express your uniqueness. In other words, there are no expectations for you to be anyone other than you.

Reflect on how safe you feel being authentic in the relationship. In what ways does the other person respect your individuality?

4. Do you take turns supporting each other?

Healthy and positive relationships are about making sure both parties feel considered and supported. There is a constant switch in roles between the giver and the taker, which lessens the emotional burden on both people. For example, when one person has a bad day, the other person is able to support them without feeling taken for granted because when it is their turn to have a bad day, the other takes on the support role.

Reflect on the balance of give and take in your relationship. First examine how well you perform both roles, then consider how well the other person performs both roles.

5. Are you able to grow together?

Another predictor of healthy and positive relationships is the shared commitment to continuous growth. Both parties accept that there is room for improvement in their relationship, which motivates them to focus on personal development, so they can be the best version of themselves.

Reflect on how much growth is a priority in your relationship. How open are you to embracing change? Provide evidence to support.

Key Takeaways

- You may not have grown up with a secure attachment style, but with the right interventions you can work toward adopting this kind of dynamic in your relationships.
- Secure relationships are based on the willingness to show and receive love. That is what makes them feel safe and validating.
- It is important to remember that you cannot build secure relationships with people who don't feel emotionally safe, such as those who are avoidant or dismissive.
- Building secure and positive relationships takes time and intentionality. Find people who share the same level of commitment to become interdependent and seek to become the best version of themselves.

Conclusion

"To be fully seen by somebody, then, and be loved anyhow—this is a human offering that can border on miraculous."

— ELIZABETH GILBERT

Ambivalent-insecure attachment, or anxious attachment, is a type of emotional bond that a parent has with their child. It naturally develops due to inconsistent nurturing that leaves a child guessing whether or not they are lovable. This bond informs how the child interacts with other people and the quality of their relationships as an adult.

If you identify as someone with anxious attachment, it is important to remind yourself that you didn't get to choose to relate to others in that way. Your attachment style came as a result of early childhood neglect or trauma that ultimately changed how you view the world and other people. Nevertheless, the responsibility to heal and rebuild your sense of self rests on you.

There is no doubt that growing up with anxious attachment has made it difficult for you to express yourself and feel safe in relationships. Throughout your childhood, and even adulthood, you may have felt desperate to hold onto unhealthy relationships that felt safe but were unresponsive to your needs. Moreover, you may have been caught off guard by the constant attachment triggers that activate upon the slightest discomfort in your relationships.

Perhaps you have reached a stage in your life where you are unwilling to continue reinforcing the same anxious patterns anymore. You may be ready to invest in relationships that allow you to be unapologetically yourself. Alternatively, you may have a strong desire to experience true love, improve your relationships with colleagues, or strengthen family connections.

This book has provided you with plenty of strategies to overcome anxious attachment. The aim of these strategies were to help you address past childhood traumas and stories, challenge the limiting beliefs that distort your understanding of relationships, heal the wounded inner child and reclaim your sense of self, as well as to reprogram your mind, so you can reinforce positive relationship behaviors.

With the knowledge and practice that you have gained from reading this book, you are equipped to finally come face-to-face with yourself and make the necessary changes to build meaningful and positive relationships. Remember to treat the process of healing anxious attachment like a journey and be patient with yourself as you reawaken aspects of you that have been hidden or invalidated for so many years. You deserve to show yourself the same love you so generously give to others!

Thank You

I really appreciate you for purchasing my book!

You had the chance to pick a lot of other books, but you chose this one.

So, **thank you so much** for purchasing this book and reading it to the very last page! I hope that I was able to help you in your healing process, as my goal is to help as many people as possible!

Before you close the book, I want to ask for **a small favor**. Would you please consider *leaving an honest review* on Amazon about the book? **This would be really helpful for me**, as I'm an independent author and posting reviews is the best and easiest way to support me.

The feedback you provide will help me so I can continue selling, improving, and writing books. **It will mean the world to me to hear from you!**

Go to this book on Amazon and scroll down (mybook.to/anxious-attachment), click on the link below or scan the QR code to leave a review:

Amazon US ——— Amazon UK ——— Rest of the World

References

Ainsworth, M. D. S., & Bell, S. M. (1970). Attachment, exploration, and separation: Illustrated by the behavior of one-year-olds in a strange situation. *Child Development, 41*(1), 49–67. https://doi.org/10.2307/11 27388

Amanda Palmer quote. (n.d.). Goodreads.

APA. (2022). *Handout 27: 5 Steps of cognitive restructuring instructions.* American Psychological Association.

Tara Bianca (November 18, 2019). *The Flower of Heaven.*

Bowlby, J. (1969). *Attachment and loss* (Vol. 1). Basic Books.

Brazelton, T. B., & Yogman, M. W. (1986). *Affective development in infancy* (pp. 95–124). Ablex Pub. Co.

Bretherton, I. (1992). The origins of attachment theory: John Bowlby and Mary Ainsworth. *Developmental Psychology, 28*(5), 759–775. https://doi.org/10.1037/0012-1649.28.5.759

Eanes, R. (2016, January 15). *Turning toward our children: Answering bids for connection.* The Gottman Institute.

Elizabeth Gilbert quote. (n.d.). Goodreads.

Harvard Health Publishing. (2020, July 6). *Understanding the stress response.* Harvard Medical School.

Henry Cloud quote. (n.d.). Goodreads.

H Raven Rose quote. (n.d.). Goodreads.

Jacobs Hendel, H. (2018, July 16). *Getting to know your three brains: Part 4 triggers.* Hilary Jacobs Hendel.

Khodabakhsh, M. (2012). Attachment styles as predictors of empathy in nursing students. *Journal of Medical Ethics and History of Medicine, 5.*

MasterClass. (2022, January 14). *Paradigm shift definition: 6 Examples of paradigm shifts.* MasterClass.

Munger, K. (n.d.). *How your attachment style impacts your stress response.* FuelEd.

Patrick Rothfuss quote. (n.d.). Goodreads.

Shelley Klammer quote. (n.d.). Goodreads.

Sinclair, J. (2021, July 12). *How mindful breathing can change your day (and your life).* BetterUp.

Sorgen, C. (n.d.). *Bonding with baby before birth.* WebMD.

Vironika Tugaleva quote. (n.d.). Goodreads.

Vishnu. (2015, May 29). *9 Ways to release your limiting beliefs so you can find love again*. Tiny Buddha.

Made in United States
Orlando, FL
08 September 2023

36838768R00118